Ecosomatics

"An utterly fascinating read; by combining personal experiences and wide-ranging research, Pallant has crafted an engaging text on finding new ways of thinking, being, and connecting. It's a much-needed call to leave distractions behind and return to your body, for our own sake and the sake of the planet."

OLIVIA CAMPBELL, NEW YORK TIMES BESTSELLING
AUTHOR OF *WOMEN IN WHITE COATS*

"With a sensitivity that sings forth, Cheryl Pallant delivers us poetry of the living body. She does this by investigating multiple facets of human nature and its interdependence with all living bodies, most notably the Earth. Dig into this inspiring book and its many pearls of bodily and emotional wisdom and opportunities for healing will unfold, centered in somatics and the ecology of how we choose to relate."

MARTHA EDDY, CMA, RSMT, ED.D, AUTHOR OF *MINDFUL
MOVEMENT* AND CREATOR OF DYNAMIC EMBODIMENT™

"Pallant's engrossing writing skillfully guides the reader to recognize connections between our physical, energetic, and intuitive selves to awaken a multidimensional sensing that informs how we may choose to interact intentionally with all aspects of life and 'a world in search of healing.'"

GINA BONDURANT, BSN, RN, CHTP, CHTI,
PRESIDENT OF HEALING BEYOND BORDERS

"This passionately articulated book shows us that in turning within we are better able to turn toward this world that desperately needs our compassionate presence. *Ecosomatics* is a wonderful guide for everyone seeking to heal the split between the personal and the planetary."

KIRK WARREN BROWN, PH.D., FACULTY MEMBER
IN THE DEPARTMENT OF PSYCHOLOGY
AT CARNEGIE MELLON UNIVERSITY AND
COEDITOR OF *HANDBOOK OF MINDFULNESS*

"Cheryl offers us a unique window into her world as an energy healer assisting people in becoming incorporated within their own earthy incarnation as a pathway to healing. Her ability to craft a sensual spell with words takes us on a rich journey through these varied perceptual layers of sensing, feeling, and understanding our place on and in the planet. She serves up many proverbial crumbs to find our way back home to a renewed wholeness."

JAMIE MCHUGH, MA, RSMT,
CREATOR OF SOMATIC EXPRESSION®

Ecosomatics

Embodiment Practices for a World in Search of Healing

A Sacred Planet Book

Cheryl Pallant

Bear & Company
Rochester, Vermont

Bear & Company
One Park Street
Rochester, Vermont 05767
www.BearandCompanyBooks.com

Bear & Company is a division of Inner Traditions International

Sacred Planet Books are curated by Richard Grossinger, Inner Traditions editorial board member and cofounder and former publisher of North Atlantic Books. The Sacred Planet collection, published under the umbrella of the Inner Traditions family of imprints, includes works on the themes of consciousness, cosmology, alternative medicine, dreams, climate, permaculture, alchemy, shamanic studies, oracles, astrology, crystals, hyperobjects, locutions, and subtle bodies.

Cataloging-in-Publication Data for this title is available from the Library of Congress

ISBN 978-1-59143-476-4 (print)
ISBN 978-1-59143-477-1 (ebook)

Printed and bound in the United States by Versa Press, Inc.

10 9 8 7 6 5 4 3 2 1

Text design and layout by Kenleigh Manseau
This book was typeset in Garamond Premier Pro with Haboro and Arquitecta used as display typefaces

To send correspondence to the author of this book, mail a first-class letter to the author c/o Inner Traditions • Bear & Company, One Park Street, Rochester, VT 05767, and we will forward the communication, or contact the author directly at **www.cherylpallant.com.**

Disaster, along with moments of social upheaval, is when the shackles of conventional belief and role fall away and the possibilities open up.

REBECCA SOLNIT

By seeing differently, we do differently.

JAMES HILLMAN

Contents

Introduction
A Shift in Consciousness

A brief burst like a released champagne cork popping against my diaphragm caught my attention. No pain accompanied it, so I easily ruled out an organ rupturing. The sensation brought up a memory of an event from my early twenties that radically shifted my perceptions and led to a few weeks of reading with a startlingly heightened comprehension of physics and biology, fields previously impenetrable and of negligible interest. I knew these events were linked, and it was time to act.

This burst came with an urgency and realization: it was time to come out and support areas of being frequently neglected and dismissed. Coming out and accepting all of who we are promotes developing latent abilities that position us in a place of strength. We confide in ourselves, then a few select others, eventually widening that circle. The root word of confide, *fid,* refers to trust. Confiding in ourselves leads to a relationship of trust, knowing, and confidence. This acceptance frees up energy previously devoted to hiding secrets and making excuses when shamed parts slipped out. Acceptance allows productive interests to come forth—we are at liberty to draw from all of our abilities. The process of accepting is as enlivening as daffodil stems breaking through the melted ground of winter to dazzle us with a hint of yellow blooms.

It comes down to accepting reality. All of reality.

The time to come out is now, because rarely does a day go by without yet another story about the ruinous impact of the climate crisis, the dysfunction of politicians, the greed and short-sightedness of the corporate community, the spread of disease, and the divisiveness of individuals. Our generation is looking at inadequate income, countless refugees, accelerated species extinction, and human decimation. These and many more unsettling events are taking place not in a hundred years, fifty, or ten, but now.

Sometimes despair clouds my day. Why phone a member of congress with a concern? Why drive an electric car? Why do away with plastic? Why go to college? Why vote? Why do anything in the face of such upheaval and what appears to be a story without a happy ending? How vital is the action of one against colossal environmental and social disruption avalanching toward destruction?

I prefer to go about my day-to-day activities against a carefree backdrop and celebrate awe in witnessing simple moments like the delivery of mail to the front door and a cardinal landing on a dogwood branch. Often I am carefree. It's a choice. For the sake of balance. For the sake of centering in heart and mind. For the sake of well-being and a healthy body, my own and that of family, friends, and strangers. For the sake of not subscribing to the paralysis that accompanies fatalism nor the flightiness that accompanies being Pollyannaish. Were I to focus attention on dire circumstances only, the weight would strangle all motivation to do anything. Despair would guide—or misguide— all decisions, and my inaction would contribute to our demise. I could look away and do nothing, but that means apathy and denial have won. Doing nothing means I've resigned myself to a sinking ship.

Yes, we're taking on water, but we can stay afloat. I turn to writing, dancing, meditating, listening to the body, healing, and serving others. These activities reinforce the importance of spontaneity, adaptability, and participation in the creative principle, the life force activated, its generative reach widespread. I turn to awakening the power of a body grounded in a purpose connected to nature outside, to dogwoods and cardinals, and to nature within. This more inclusive nature also involves tapping into abilities previously sidelined. For solutions, balance, and sustainability to be mainstays and for viable systems to emerge, we must let go of what no longer works—or what only works for a few at the expense of the many—for processes that do.

A perilous moment such as our current one is a call for us to shift our consciousness, to awaken and cultivate who we are, to heal personal and collective wounds, to uncover latent and dismissed abilities, and to embrace a broader range of sensory and perceptive abilities. The times call for examining and letting go of limiting habits and beliefs and instead embracing ourselves as richly multidimensional beings. The times ask us to be more honest and authentic and to transform. It's a recognition of the need for growth, expanded awareness, and integration that positively impacts health and well-being, not exclusively for oneself but for all sentient and insentient beings, life acknowledged as interconnected. It's a recognition that if despair and stress dominate, cortisol floods the body and we are less resilient, susceptible to chronic ailments, less available, too, for problem-solving, creative expression, compassion, love, and awe. It's a recognition of the value of feeling vulnerable, perched at a growth edge that may topple us toward suffering or tilt us toward a cohesion of an interdependent self that is vibrantly alive and enthusiastic about tomorrow. It's a choice.

We're on the cusp of personal and collective change, one an extension of the other, a developmental step that, when faced with a more complete range of our abilities, furthers human potential. Consider the time we are in as an invitation to live with an open heart, alert mind, and dynamic integration of our being grounded in our body in alliance with family, community, and Earth. It's how we thrive.

A moment such as this challenges us to live from a passion and higher purpose that includes offering abilities to the greater good. You deserve it. I deserve it. We deserve it. To make what is possible within reach.

Connections are everywhere, perceivable when we open our minds and hearts and feel into the greater field of our being. Knowingly and unknowingly we are all transmitting our joys and fears, compassionate responses as well as damaging reactivity. Now is the time to be intentional and choose compassion, connection, collaboration, and growth. Now is the time to hone awareness to orient us to new realizations and expansive, heightened states of consciousness. Now is the time to celebrate embodied presence, flow, respect for all beings, and the flourishing of life.

My hope is that the ideas, stories, and exercises in this book break us out of limited thinking and perceiving in exchange for new possibilities and we wake up from the illusion of our separateness. My hope is that we step out of a common egocentric perspective for another view. How about ecocentric? Biocentric? Somatocentric? Cosmocentric?

This book aims to contribute to an evolutionary shift in consciousness that embraces well-being for all. All hands need to be on deck, which means all ideas, including the marginalized and ridiculed, are to be considered. Wisdom asks us to look past dogma and entertain curiosity to uncover a greater depth of sensory awareness, effective processes, level-headed and imaginatively bold, intuitive responses. It asks us to recognize how little we understand what is around us and how superficially we venture within. It asks us to reside more compassionately with our body, to feel its many wonders, and perceive the previously obscured. Increasing awareness and deepening embodiment connects us to, well, everything.

We all have the spark that takes underutilized and hidden abilities to illuminate a mind. Taking action is a recognition that contributing to a positive outcome matters. It means faith rather than despondency, help rather than horror, love rather than fear, and giving balanced with taking. Ideas like interdependence, entrainment, and quantum entanglement point toward collective interactivity—how every action, thought, and feeling influences the whole. Missing in any given moment may be knowing the specifics of the connection or an outcome. Waiting for specifics, however, is a luxury previous generations may have been able to afford, but not us, and not now. As environmental activist Greta Thunberg said in a 2018 address to a UN conference on climate change, "I am here to say, our house is on fire . . . I want you to act as you would in a crisis. I want you to act as if our house is on fire. Because it is." The raging fire is claiming the land, water, air, schools, jobs, homes, and our physical and mental health. We don't have the luxury to wait if we want a heartful, habitable future. By honoring the spark and dwelling compassionately in our body in the present moment, infinite possibilities appear.

This is a book about transformative change, expanded knowing and heightened consciousness, about becoming whole. It's about opening ourselves to enhanced human ability. It's about embracing a potential greater than our family or culture may have led us to believe can happen. It's about broadening the foundation of who we are, increasing awareness, and moving from personal bias and cultural blind spots into wisdom and new abilities. It's about healing personal and cultural wounds, redefining the body, expanding awareness, and stepping fearlessly into our being. It's about connecting with a shifting consciousness. To handle the challenges before us, we need all options and skills placed on the table, our mind working in congruence with our heart, an embodied integrative intelligence in coherence with nature.

The times call for reflection and growth. These values mark the difference between reactivity and responsiveness, thoughtlessness and compassion, constriction and freedom. They lead to benefits like adaptability, resiliency, love, and inventiveness. They reveal an interconnected web that couples person to person to animal to insect to water to soil to air to cloud to star, all as limitless, unfathomable, and awesome. This web reveals options and choices that contribute to establishing new synaptic paths, embodied presence, a vitalizing, integrated presence, and healthy environment—essentially a way forward.

What's being called for is letting go of habits that no longer serve us in favor of ones that uplift and deliver us into a favorable tomorrow. We are teetering at a growth edge that is unprecedented. This edge is rife with danger; it's also an epic opportunity. What happens next depends on how we direct our attention, what we believe, and what actions we take. There is no greater opportunity than the one upon us. Now is a turning point, a threshold, a place of power, an opening to flow, presence, and emergence.

A central theme running throughout these pages is a focus on the body. Do we *have* a body? Is it a commodity like a car? Do we live *in* a body in the same way we live in an apartment or house? How these questions are answered depends on the background of the respondent. Generally speaking, a medical doctor may define the body as a combination of chemicals, hormones, organs, bones, and breath, with thought a function of brain activity. This mechanistic view contrasts with the view of a theologian who may refer to the body as spirit or thought as a reflection of divine influence. The difference explains why an altered state of consciousness may be regarded by a doctor as a brain phenomenon or chemical imbalance, whereas a theologian may regard it as an inspired vision. As a somatic practitioner with a history of dance, meditation, and energy healing, I tend to avoid dualistic, reductive thinking in favor of exploring the richness of subjective experience. Attentiveness to bodily presence using both narrow and wide lenses reveals details frequently overlooked and cultivates a refined awareness of emotion, sensation, and thought. To be intimately in touch with the rhythms of one's body ushers in a sense of belonging and empowered knowing. We come to know the many events taking place within our skin while also recognizing this membrane as a porous and ever-moving boundary. By connecting with sensations, emotions, and thoughts as they arise, fall away, or remain, the terrain of a body in constant flux, we connect with our personal body with its many idiosyncrasies. We investigate the limitless range of the body's abilities.

Notably, a body is in continuous dialogue with the environment, an awareness that has given birth to ecosomatics. This emergent field, which combines somatics with ecology, recognizes the personal body as inextricable from the planetary body. Our body is part of the global ecosystem. Or said another way, the ecology of our body is part of the ecology of earth. Nature is not outside us. It is not the woods or mountains accessed only when we walk out the door of our home. We are nature. We are water, earth, fire, and air. We are cells, microbes, and bacteria. We are in relationship with everything around us, from a computer to a glass of water to clouds and a neighbor's dog. The understanding of this interrelatedness shows how nature is inseparable from who we are.

Ecosomatics encourages us to ground in our body along with the body of earth. It encourages us to heighten our senses to increase our innate natural intelligence. It asks us to place awareness on the ecology of our body tied to the flesh of earth. As we weather dramatic environmental changes and investigate what sustains us, we are urged to show up in our body more responsively and engage ecosomatic listening that puts us in touch with all of nature.

Of particular interest are the experiences that disrupt habitual ways of sensing and perceiving, which lead to challenging assumptions. Disruptions are a crossroad, an occasion of heightened senses and thought, consciousness asked to reorient. Hopefully what takes place is a period or journey of reflection and integration of the experience into a fresh understanding, a revision of a belief system that includes this new information. This journey, when done with mindful curiosity and self-compassion, involves refining senses and shifting awareness. Such journeys, not always easy or quick, are well worth the pursuit. They are the path of growth, healing, becoming whole, and recognizing our transpersonal nature. They lead to new levels of human potential, ego maturity, elevated states of consciousness, and a transpersonal purpose that sees an individual self as vital as the myriad beings that inhabit the planet.

This book is full of personal stories as well as anecdotes from clients. Some stories on healing and anomalous visions are less easily explicable than others. To understand the invisible mechanisms working behind the scenes, I turn to psychology, sociology, quantum physics, and neurobiology, yet I realize they go only so far as all perspectives, or perceptual filters, do. My attempts to explain them are full of logistic holes. Logic, like any filter, as necessary as it is, only portrays a partial truth, one we have come to accept as the be-all and end-all despite its shortcomings. This acceptance eclipses other understandings and ways of knowing, like the somatic, intuitive, energetic, and feminine intelligences this book elaborates on and encourages.

I share this book with you and ask you to suspend your cynic. I ask, too, that you suspend your champion eager to buy into ideas wholesale. Neither the cynic nor the zealot taps fully into Truth. Neither grounds us in personal, embodied knowing. Neither honors feeling into the totality of who we are. My suggestion is that we notice bodily sensations, thoughts, and beliefs, and consider how they color perception. Witness what is taking place in the body in the present moment. Question assumptions and investigate without bias when feasible. Suspend habits and practice trust in felt experience. Uncover flow and establish balance. In doing so, nuanced perceptions rooted in a personal body connect us to innate wisdom. One hand holds knowing while the other hand holds unknowing. A book such as this asks us to use both hands. It encourages aligning with the energy of our body tied to the energy beyond our skin. It encourages accessing conscious and unconscious bodily events that can lead to improved stewardship to ourselves and the planet.

* * *

That this book rests in your hands suggests that your heart, mind, spirit, and energy are ready to shift—or further the shift already underway. The shift is for your sake, your family, friends, community, and the planet—ambitious claims, I admit. No pressure though. Only notice. Only witness the awe that is life unfolding within and around you.

1

The Roots of Beliefs

*You understand so little of what is around you because you
do not use what is within you.*

ST. HILDEGARD VON BINGEN

During the summer prior to my senior year of college, I attended a writing class through the New Haven Arts Council. The instructor and classmates, older than me with spouses, children, and jobs in fields like law, city government, education, and social work, all provided helpful instruction on voice, structure, and revision. A visitor joined the class halfway through one evening, took an available seat and, unlike the rest of us, listened without taking notes. As class ended and we collected our belongings to head home, he invited us to his apartment across the street.

We gladly climbed the stairs to his top floor apartment to snack on chips and fruit placed on the kitchen counter. We chatted about class, their jobs, and my schooling until one by one everyone left. Except me. I felt compelled to stay and meandered over to an unfinished painting leaning against a wall. Something about its dark, misty shades of red and blue, with a ladder rising up from the center, stirred me in an unfamiliar way. "Not finished," said the host who I learned was the painter and a physics professor.

We had not previously discussed the painting. In fact, we had not talked with each other at all. As I gazed at the picture, my mind flashed on the images he'd be including in the painting. I shared the details with him.

"How did you know that?" he asked.

I didn't. Or not in the usual sense of knowing where the information source is easily trackable. For instance, there were no sketches or magazine cutouts on a nearby table and no overheard conversations about the painting. The images suddenly appeared in my mind along with a gut sense of knowing.

He invited me to sit. He wanted to know more. I took a chair across from him on the couch, which is when the strangeness of my sight took a turn into stranger. As I settled into the cushion of the chair and met his eyes, another series of images launched.

Events from my life appeared in my mind, not select events, but every family encounter, every day in school since kindergarten, every visit with a friend in the neighborhood, every conversation with parents and brothers. These events cataloged my entire life and appeared as simultaneously playing movie clips situated side by side and atop another in a conical shape. I, or my awareness unclouded by emotion or attitude, stood in the center at the narrow part of this cone, a vantage point that let me look multiple directions and choose where to look. An entire episode was viewable with the turn of my attention. The focus of my attention included not only my original perspective and understanding of the event, but also the perspective of the participants for which I did not have previous access. Here was my history but also a record of their thoughts and attitude. If I loosened my focus on the event, other narratives and interpretations showed up, missing pieces I hadn't known were missing. Here, too, was incredible insight and knowing, which I felt bodily with an unfamiliar ease. No words accurately capture the experience. Spellbound, dumbfounded, startled, awakened, shifted?

The simultaneously playing reels of my life did not end with my viewing. A commanding voice invited me to ask questions. The voice came with no physical body but was purely a vocal presence. From my neutral central space, I knew, in the same way I knew about the images forthcoming in the painting, that the voice had a comprehensive understanding of my life and that it would be advisable to take advantage of it by asking pivotal questions and not waste the moment on small talk. I asked why I struggled with depression. The voice responded, "You're not being yourself, but what others want you to be." I asked other questions including ones about writing. With each question, the voice replied with unquestionable resonant clarity.

At some point the cone—and I use this term lightly, unable to find a better word—disappeared and my awareness returned to the painter seated across from me. I didn't know how long I was gone, a few seconds or an hour, and if I missed any of his talking, but my host did not mention glazed eyes, slumping in the chair, or any other telltale sign. He sat cross-legged, his arms resting on the chair undisturbed, as if blinking and breathing were the sole extent of my activity, not falling through an inexplicable portal. I felt uncomfortable bringing up my experience, politely mentioned the late hour, and departed for home to write deep into the evening.

The next day, I went to the library—this was before the internet—to attempt to understand what happened. Without proper search terms, "bizarre" and "freaky" leading nowhere, I flipped through many unhelpful books. But something else odd was taking place. When thumbing through science books that I dubiously pulled from the shelves, I absorbed complex concepts that previously would have taken hours to understand, let alone capture my interest. My mind processed them readily as if they were common ideas like a mouse or sleep, so it was a stack of these books that accompanied me home.

A few weeks later, my easy absorption of scientific ideas disappeared like a light switched to the off position. One moment there was ease of comprehension and the next moment: zap, gone. I flipped open the books and turned the pages, but the ideas had taken on an impenetrable density, and I no longer had the patience to slog through them. Worst of all, none of the reading increased my understanding of what had taken place, and I couldn't think of anyone to ask. The books got returned, slipped into the bin at the front desk of the library, their pages ready for the next patron. But there was no turning back for me. There was an aftereffect like a sunburn, the skin still hot long past sunset, yet there was no discomfort, only curiosity. It led me to linger longer than was customary on someone's face, their words and actions, to question my own impressions, aware not to take any conclusion at face value, any understanding a likely mask or decoy to other perspectives.

THE VALUE OF BEING AUTHENTIC

Practicing authenticity is challenging for anyone regardless of age. Authenticity requires us to recognize discrete sensations, emotions, and thoughts. It requires developing somatic and emotional intelligences. Is the throat tickle from pollen or irritation with our colleague at work, for instance? Do we want to pack up the house to move or stay put and renovate? What is the source for being tired or moody or anxious? How do we respond to a challenging situation without losing balance and integrity? Authenticity requires noting the firm and fluid boundaries separating self from a group that may be familial, social, civic, or national. Authenticity leads to noticing that a self is not constant and solid, but in continuous flux with multiple identifiers and labels, a process influenced by causes and conditions while also acting as an influencer. Authenticity as a two-way street leads to understanding *self* and *body* as verbs, not only nouns, that we self and body our way through life. We are the active embodiment of influencing and being influenced.

Conformity has its rewards. We can kick back in compliance with known rules and standards and not have to invent habits and behaviors from scratch. We can let someone else assume the lead while we nod in agreement and find a comfortable enough spot to fit in. We can participate in maintaining a preestablished order and feel the security and support that comes with belonging to a group. We are not ostracized as the rebel or outsider or another label meant to belittle, shame, and bully us into joining in. We can refrain from devoting endless hours or years of reflection to determine what is authentic and what is pretentious. A society relies upon a high number of its citizens complying to its norms, be it traffic laws that most of us gladly follow or niceties like saying "sorry" if we accidentally bump elbows. Conformity reinforces order and discourages mayhem. It provides a welcome safety net.

Conformity has a downside. We may never find out who we are if we're feeding the needs of others while neglecting our own. We may squeeze ourselves to fit in despite a mismatch to the detriment of our health, well-being, and potential. We may abandon critical thinking and go along with a group regardless of the value or morality of the actions. History contains plenty of examples of groupthink in which individuals followed the customs and beliefs of a group and reconsidered their actions only in retrospect, after heinous actions took place and someone pointed a finger to more virtuous principles. Consider the Salem witch trials or the lynching of African Americans.

If conformity is our north star, we may have no inkling about nor ability to cultivate our highest self. We may blind ourselves to developing new technology, the cure for dementia, the ability to find love, or the needed action to make the world sustainable. We may be oblivious to the habits and ideas that are in our worst or best interests, unable to recognize the distinction between them. We may believe life happens to us, be a passive player, and have yet to see our part in the drama, the choices made and those awaiting. We don't realize the difference between writing the script versus reading the role cast by another.

The *eccentric*, a term for the conformist's opposite, is the one who relationally stands outside the circle, guided by her own set of rules. These are highly individualistic people who see problems from unexpected angles and conjure innovative solutions or create moving works of art. They are the leaders, the inventors, the artists, mystics, and entrepreneurs. Think Einstein, Mozart, Madame Curie, Susan B. Anthony, Steve Jobs, James Baldwin, Remedios Varo, Rachel Carson. They are the visionaries who dare take imaginative leaps. They are pioneers compelled to follow their instincts and willing to go it alone without the support of their peers. The eccentric is labeled *unconventional, quirky, weird,* terms that may be favorable or unfavorable depending on your upbringing and self-esteem. Interesting that the word *weird,* which carries a negative connotation, was originally considered a moniker of great strength. *Weird* derives from Old English *wyrd* meaning "fate, chance, and destiny" and is defined as "having power to control fate," a quality that I consider an enviable superpower to have access to. Weird implies authenticity. Authenticity includes self-reliance and self-empowerment.

Among the strengths of living authentically is a sense of liberty. Freedom comes from being your own boss, following your own hunches and inclinations, and assuming responsibility. We get to draw from our individualized knowing based on firsthand experience and reflection that provide the confidence and ease to make decisions. Enlivened, energized, and uplifted, we are attentive to both our personal world and the larger world. We sense and reflect, look outside ourselves and within. Personal power, our inner strength and intelligences, informs us about when to push forward and when to retreat, when to voice up and when to listen, when to follow the gut feeling and when to wait or leap, and when to strategize or sit back and watch clouds.

It is not an either/or situation but a matter of how much of one and in what combination and balance. It's a matter of ongoing inquiry and investigation. It's a matter of knowing that a moment's conclusion is not absolute, but one among many, any of which may reveal itself with time, a brightening light, or a late-night journaling.

IT'S A MATTER OF PERSPECTIVE

Reflecting on my visit to the painter's apartment, I recognize the importance of attention. Where I turned my attention, my focus, influenced my perspective. I offer another word: *filter*. We have innumerable filters operating every second, many simultaneously. A filter is a way we define ourselves that directly influences perception. Filters are the way we interpret experience, draw conclusions, and make meaning. Some examples of filters: daughter, mother, American, patriot, construction worker, cashier, vacationer, retiree, optimist, cynic, entitled, victim. These filters, many based on occupation, are easily identifiable. The filters that are more difficult to define come from beliefs tied to motivation and consequent actions. With beliefs, we move into territory about what is conscious and what is unconscious along with the blurry line between them. For instance, we believe we deserve a rewarding job unlike our current one, consider filling in applications, yet we can't muster the enthusiasm to do so and blame the inaction on poor sleep. Sleep factors in, of course, but the lack of enthusiasm may suggest an unconscious belief operating in the background that sabotages our best interests. Or we may say we believe in God yet never attend a formal service, rationalizing our lack of attendance as not having enough time. Conscious beliefs conceal unconscious ones, awareness going only so far in any given moment. We may happily water the plants in the house yet not recognize what led to tripping on the leg of a chair and dinging our knee on a table, not once, but twice, careless actions quickly written off as accidental despite their being a call to increase or redirect our attention. We may want to watch where blame gets cast and ensure we are not acting out of insecurity, shame, or an unconscious motive that could lead to a hasty and inappropriate accusation, a reaction that overlooks actual cause, only its deflection.

Filters bias perceptions. A woman who identifies as a mother may look at a crowd and notice the children and how attentively parents hold their children's hands. The mother may overlook the people wearing sports shoes because her filter excludes being athletic. Similarly she may not notice the cowlicks of people nearby, a detail a hairdresser would readily see. If she is grieving a child lost from a miscarriage, she may focus on the healthy children and envy smiling parents.

At any given moment there are infinite details to perceive. For instance, as I write, my focus is obviously on the flow of thoughts pertinent to this narrative. I'm aware of the chosen background music of a woman chanting and my belly sated by my recent lunch. When I take a step back, my awareness shifts to the placement of my feet on the floor, the angle (just corrected) of my body on the chair, and the stack of student papers awaiting grades. A few more minutes reveals heat at my neck, concern about a friend in the hospital, and a desire to check in on him. By necessity we focus on minimal consciously selected details to avoid bombarding the nervous system with sensory input, feeling overwhelmed, and getting little done. Even then, distractions continually get in the way.

Utilized filters not only influence our perceptions but also consequent conclusions and decisions. I am not singing, for instance. I am not phoning the hospital. Nor am I mothering unless my nurturing of words is considered motherly. I don't know which pen I'll use to grade. Yet to be determined, too, is knowing if the ink of my chosen pen has dried up, which would cause me to riffle through the drawer for a replacement or dash to the store and the appropriate aisle. Cause-effect-cause-effect ad infinitum.

It's challenging to go filter-free, to perceive from a place of neutrality or clear seeing, to watch what arises in each moment. This means regarding as equal a circumstance typically considered positive (receiving a tender text from a beloved) from a negative (a bill collector knocking at the door). However, it is worth suspending one or two attachments to experiment with what else comes into view.

Try This

Commit to a finite manageable period, perhaps an hour or a day, to experiment. Choose to approach all situations neutrally. Greet whatever presents itself—a flat tire, a one-hundred-dollar bill on the sidewalk, endless waiting for a technician on the phone, an email from a close friend—as if the incident is neither welcome nor unwelcome. Consider it neutral information that is neither good nor bad. Let go of expectation. Respond from your highest self with integrity and authenticity. Welcome curiosity. Watch how the incident unfolds. How does your response and the outcome differ from having an attached attitude?

Any perception is bound to be incomplete, which means that our take or someone else's perception, including those that run counter to ours, may be as true as our own, the glass both half full and half empty. It's easy to entertain me being right and you being wrong, the preferred arrangement, the ego often skewing details of a situation to situate us having the upper hand. It takes maturity to recognize and admit to being mistaken. It takes a broadened perspective to recognize how we may both be right—or wrong. Imagination is needed to see how we both have a handle on truth, despite another's unfamiliar angle. Here lies an area of growth and potential, an area of exploration, if we choose to regard it as such.

BIAS

The episode in the painter's apartment resembles traits of a life review, what frequently coincides with a near-death experience, when events of one's life are evaluated, oftentimes providing access to new perspectives. A near-death experience is usually provoked by a sudden accident or prolonged illness. Many who return from death's door share accounts of accessing the library of their existence, meeting deceased relatives, approaching a supernal light or godlike figure, and revising their attitude or life purpose. For me, there was no illness, death, light, ancestors and, for those wondering, no alcohol or drugs. There was a dramatic scene change, an all-knowing voice, and access to a vast storehouse of knowledge.

In my narrative of this episode, notice my previous avoidance of common terms such as *life review* and *near-death experience*. This is not an example of coyness but of seeking appropriate terms as does any writer who rolls word after word on her tongue in search of the right one. But my quest for the mot juste goes further than literary craft. Words, especially nouns, are powerful filters. They imply a settled notion. Their very presence on the line, or from the mouth, slants our thinking, some inclinations more incendiary than others. It's hard to unsee written words or unhear what's been said. Word choice contains associated ideas and—this is the part to watch for—our judgments about them. Consider *donut,* which we know is a small ring-shaped fried cake of sweetened dough. That's the neutral information. Here's where it gets interesting. Reading the word *donut* may have prompted some of us to salivate. Oh, we think happily, there's that donut shop with our favorite chocolate one with raspberry frosting near the bank that we're going to later. Why not indulge our sweet tooth? Mentioning a donut to the health and weight conscious among us may conjure condemnation because these sweet cakes are caloric, sugary, and lack nutrition. Some may be irritated at me for mentioning the doughy delight because of a shortage of willpower to avoid what is now craved. My apology if you're among the latter.

Let me throw out several more words unrelated to dessert and watch the lights of your filters flicker: *telepathy, psychic, ESP, precognition, soul, psi, remote viewing, hyperreal, paranormal, New Age, transcendent.* Here are some others: *whimsy, direct, pointed, futuristic, mystical, presence.* By now your senses are in a spin, your judgments fanned, the lights of your filter in slow or quick strobe.

Obviously words are effective in communication. They're necessary for sharing information. They're the messengers that deliver a bounty of goods from one mind to another. The sender intends us to receive the message fully intact, free of the dents, dings, and tears of misunderstanding. If we do discover damage, we can ask a follow-up question for clarity. For the sake of broadening understanding, my intent is to convey the details of my story as accurately as possible with a minimum of misleading filters. Too many of the words associated with this event and others to be shared in the following pages are susceptible to judgment, and I want to open minds, not close them, to increase ability and potential, and get us to perceive what was previously imperceptible. Says poet William Blake, "If the doors of perception were cleansed every thing would appear to man as it is, Infinite. For man has closed himself up, till he sees all things thro' narrow chinks of his cavern."[1]

Among the filters in play that many of us rely upon are dualism and binary thinking. We say dark or light, confusing or clear, happy or sad, and so on. This filter of dualism is pervasive in the language used in describing something as this or that, a language pattern you'll find ample examples of in these pages because they effectively hone an idea. In many cases, their presence is benign enough. It gets more complicated when used to address more complex, nuanced ideas. Consider ideas related to consciousness and modes of knowing, commonly framed oppositionally as, for instance, science versus religion, intellect versus imagination, reality versus delusion, or the pros and the cons, to name several. Where is both or a third or a plenitude of possibility? Where is a more comprehensive frame? What gets lost perceptually because our choices are limited? Comparative religion professor and writer Joseph Campbell refers to dualism cloaked in the myth of Adam and Eve as our prime fall. He says, "Male and female, life and death, good and evil: problems of opposites. The trouble that began was the discovery of duality. That was the Fall. There was no recognition of duality before this."[2]

Among other rules, language guidelines encourage minimizing the size of a list. For the sake of clear communication, writing manuals recommend limiting a list to about three items, to write this, that, and another, and then to stop. Such manuals also recommend sentence length be about twenty-five words to avoid confusing a reader. Of course there are many exceptions by writers who eloquently defy the recommendation. James Joyce's Molly Bloom's dreamy soliloquy in *Ulysses* comes in at 3,687 words, and a sentence in Martin Luther King's moving "Letter from Birmingham Jail" comes in at 345 words.

Unless going for literary effect, we are often discouraged from writing a sentence like the following: I spend the afternoon sitting back, pondering with, then without a cup of coffee, crossing my left leg over the right, one foot on the floor, the left foot dangling like a question mark while I grab my journal, whose pages await the ink of my words and doodles, and I peer out the window at a car pulling into a tight spot, a poor fit for an untrained parker, and only later do I walk in the garden, step on a twig from the ailanthus tree, its snap underfoot reverberating up my spine as I consider making dinner, wonder about the freshness of garlic, turmeric, and chives in the cabinet and whether a trip to the store needs to happen this afternoon or what needs to happen in the big picture, this sentence an example of my preference for streams of details, lushness with twists and rhythmic patterns more common to poetry, also a sentence that a prose or newspaper editor would likely recommend I cut into bite-size morsels. Do not task the reader, the editor would likely suggest. Don't make us work hard. Get to the point. What happens when getting to the point and making it easy for the reader also biases the reader, when you know that what gets written implies and occludes the unwritten? Writing is, after all, often a translation of experience one step removed from the actual event, the essence of the original hopefully contained within the scatter of letters and words crafted on the page.

Bias is inevitable, of course. The words chosen and those left off the line influence what we perceive or don't. Reading between or beyond the lines isn't a common practice, except for the poetically and syntactically dexterous among us whose hermeneutic eye and mind simultaneously hold the word, symbol, essence, rhythm, overlays, underpinnings, and multiple meanings without being knocked off balance and spilling any of it. Sometimes a fish is just a fish. Other times the connotations and effort are exactly what is needed to spark learning, the wriggling, scaly, inscribed creature creating a mental squirm. Difficulty can spur new ability. Confusion can stimulate new understanding. Challenge can break us open. Obviously details and careful word choice matter greatly, along with associated words that generate an additional loop of meaning. While reading, I sometimes wonder what edited story lines and rejected words litter the writer's floor.

THE POWER OF WITNESSING

How do we get to what's really happening, to what's really there, whatever There may be? Sometimes we reach it through poetry. Says poet and Zen priest Wendy Lewis in her poem "It's Like This," "There's this bird/And you catch it in your hands/You feel its softness, warmth, its heart/rapidly beating/But if you keep holding it it's no/longer a bird/So you open your hands/(Catch it and let it go/again and again)."[3]

Perhaps we reach it through silence.

Just this:

Or through slight motion.

Yet we're used to moving from one word to the next, one conversation or thought or task to the next, one hour or week or month to the next, and the categories any of them fall into. What gets overlooked are the experiences and perceptions that do not fit. These are the outliers, the anomalies, the exceptions, the seemingly empty moments in between. These are the Not Yet Known, the As Yet to Be Defined, the pause or gap, the contradictory and paradoxical, the undeveloped areas of potential. These spaces may make us uncomfortable given our preference for knowing and the security that comes with it. These areas challenge us to think outside familiar categories and beyond a dualistic frame. They may be neither this nor that but something else altogether. There awaits a neutral space, an emergent space, the moment between that is neither the exhale nor the inhale. Perhaps both and something more.

Just this.

We sense. We witness.

The experience at the painter's apartment was not my first experience that showed a shortfall of understanding. Many years earlier while I was in grade school, a curious incident occurred with my aunt Corrine, my grandmother's beloved sister.

From the kitchen on the ground floor, my parents and grandparents murmured. They likely conversed in words with separate voices but the stairs and hallway formed a buffer from me silently clutching the edge of the daybed upstairs. My fingers pressed the lip of the cover, a rounded seam that yielded to my constant squeezes. In the next room, my grandfather's study doubling as a guest room, my aunt moaned with guttural resonance. She voiced no words, the effort to form them no longer at her command.

I did not understand what was going on, not fully. She was sick, breast cancer having spread to her lymph glands. She had no energy to interact.

Aunt Corrine had no children or husband. She worked as a secretary in the Empire State Building in Manhattan. I sometimes visited her in her studio apartment with a bed that folded up astonishingly to become wall, a Murphy bed, a name as yet unknown to me. We sometimes sat at the counter at the Chock full o'Nuts diner, my legs too short to reach the footrest, so she could drink coffee and I could gulp milk for our shared apple pie. Before visiting my parents, brothers, and me in Connecticut, she'd phone to see if I wanted her to visit, always yes. I'd stand expectantly at the station, my eyes straining to glimpse the train arriving from the bend on the northbound track.

We played Scrabble, an activity contributing to my interest in language. She introduced me to peculiar words like *id* and demonstrated how the I and D tiles fit adjacent to other words already on the board to increase her score. As we took turns placing tiles on the board, she'd ask about school or friends, her presence in the house filling me with joy.

The night at my grandparents' New York home as she lay in bed, my joy leaked away, replaced by confusion and fear. From the room beside hers, I listened to wave after wave of her moans echoing throughout my torso. I wanted to enter her room and sit on the bed as I might have done when she was healthy, but a heaviness held me back. When I finally gathered enough nerve, I slipped off the bed, tiptoed to the doorway of her room, and perched at the threshold looking but not wanting to look, wanting to sit beside her but unable to take another step. Her body puddled under the blanket; her head turned toward the wall. A gray-blue fog filled the room despite a soft, warm light from the lamp at the bedside table. Unable to press past the doorway, I retreated back to the daybed. An hour later my parents, brothers, and I got into the car for the ninety-minute ride home.

Her kiss on the cheek woke me up. She woke me to say goodbye. She stroked my head. I glanced at the clock: 2:00 a.m. Then I fell back asleep.

At breakfast my grandmother phoned to say Aunt Corrine died at two in the morning. "I know," I said to my mom. "She visited me last night."

No response.

Grief is like that. We don't know what to say. Numbness acts as an unhappy filler in the face of loss. The pained heart cracks and out tumbles shards and rubble. But this was another type of silence, an ignoring. My mentioning her early morning visit to a few others the following weeks led to a similar response. It was as if I'd said nothing. As if I never stood in the doorway or awoke in bed. As if no such illness can take a life. Or perhaps it was the usual dismissal of the experiences of a young girl.

GREETING DISCOMFORT

This was my first encounter with death. I learned that cancer stops the body from functioning and a grieving family makes phone calls to talk slowly and sometimes not at all. I learned that biting the inside of my cheek, a habit I adopted from my aunt, upset my mother who yelled at me to stop. It did not occur to me to question whether Aunt Corrine's appearance at my bedside was normal in the same way I did not question the funeral arrangements.

I had yet to understand death or loss or possibility. I grappled with the absence of her phone calls, the loss of my Scrabble partner, but mostly I missed the gleam in her eyes. I had yet to encounter a study by researcher W. D. Rees who interviewed nearly three hundred widows and widowers and found that nearly half of them were visited by their spouse after death, love strong enough to bridge the gap between the living and the deceased.[4]

About the same time, a friend's father died from a massive heart attack. Her mom told me he was now "peacefully up in the clouds." I didn't ask how he got there: by ladder, escalator, or another form of transport. When I took my first flight soon after, I plastered my face to the airplane window eager to wave to my aunt, my friend's father, and whoever else floated peacefully above, unsure if they'd be sitting in rocking chairs or lounging on their side pillowed by a small cumulus cloud.

The airplane pierced the clouds, which, as you know and my young mind did not, revealed none of the peacefully passed doing whatever one does upon migrating to the billows of condensed watery vapors. I sank disappointedly into my seat and did not look out the window again until landing.

I took the words of my neighbor's mom literally. How many other mistruths and lies did adults tell, my young mind wondered. I had yet to understand figurative talk, euphemisms, mistakes, white lies, and deceit. I had yet to recognize the influence of beliefs and what the body can or cannot do.

Life happens. We reflect, categorize, and draw conclusions about events that sit well enough at the table beside other beliefs. Most of us want security, acceptance by a group, respect, and a decent paycheck. We may welcome challenging experiences that turn our thinking upside down and reveal truth in its shimmering glory or reject such fissures that rupture our heart and thought. Isn't there enough to focus on with work, family, and the day's demands?

A settled mind provides comfort. It's nothing to be scoffed at. It provides a welcome consistency and predictability. We can maneuver through the day with a minimum of strain. As does a closed mind, especially since a closed mind doesn't see itself as such. Even those of us who complain repeatedly about a situation may not question any underlying problematic belief nor recognize our power to alter our response or situation.

Ignorance is bliss until it isn't, until the coddling belief and conditioning intended as comfort is shown to be a prison. Some prisoners don't recognize the bars or don't identify the key holders as themselves.

Besides, who needs to look if we have sufficient food, shelter, and margarita mix? Effort is, well, effortful. Complacency is easy.

THE SAFETY OF BELIEFS

Beliefs give us safe harbor when the seas churn and we want a dry, calm shelter. They're the ointment that dulls the sting of grief. They're the ballast for the tumult of confusion. They're the story that helps us fall asleep.

Beliefs let us go about the day's business without fretting about whether gravity might reverse its pull. They help us plan a family, decide where to establish a new business, and determine what color to paint a room. Given to us by family, friends, religion, and schooling, they form the fabric of a household, neighborhood, community, and country. They work behind the scenes and in the foreground, informing decisions about work, leisure, living, and dying. They creep like vines into what we think, feel, and perceive.

Here are some common beliefs and possible conclusions related to the passing of my aunt:

- I was a quiet child. I did not speak up emphatically enough to cut through my parents' preoccupations.
- My parents never heard me.
- Death is an uncomfortable and frightening reality. We hide weakening bodies away in sanitized hospitals. My grandparents welcomed my aunt into their home, but her dying was still challenging and sad.
- Cancer is the big scary *C,* like a monster that creates havoc, one we engage in battle.
- At the time, little research had been devoted to women's health, especially on a sexualized part of the body like breasts.
- Death means it's time for heaven or hell.
- Death means it's time for reincarnation.

- The body consists of approximately 72 percent water. Oxygen and hydrogen, among other elements, play a significant role in the composition of our body. Remove all water and our solid remains could fit into one hand. The density of our matter is not as dense as our appearance suggests.
- The body is a temple.
- The body is the home of sin.
- No part of the body continues after the final breath.
- The soul or a form of consciousness persists after death.
- Experiences like dying allow consciousness to expand beyond usual bounds.
- Spirits do not exist. People who see them are loony.
- *Spirit* is a common word for a collection of nonphysical electromagnetic energy.
- Children have great imaginations and readily make up stories.
- Children readily tune in to phenomena adults have been conditioned away from perceiving.

At best, beliefs work in tandem with knowledge, facts, and experiences that lay out a path that frees us to focus on what requires our immediate attention. Beliefs provide a helpful and necessary function. But at some point their functionality can prove ineffective, problematic, even harmful, particularly when minds close, senses are refuted, and evidence is discarded, when we listen to the stories of a select group and refuse to adapt to changing conditions, when all we know is No or Yes and there is no room for Maybe or I'll Look Into It Later, and we overlook the value of connecting to our personal body.

Prior to beliefs and among their underpinnings are firsthand, felt experiences, the senses alert to various bodily phenomenon detected by touch, smell, sight, hearing, and taste. Senses provide pivotal information for navigating how we walk, drive, eat, sleep, work, and become a responsible adult. However, a cultural emphasis upon thought and objective knowledge reinforced in school eclipses refining sensory awareness and connecting with the body's cues. Superficial awareness of bodily phenomena numbs us to its activity and limits acknowledging who we are. There's a tendency to disparage the body. Many of us unfairly refer to the body as something we lug around. It requires daily maintenance of food and sleep and is rarely as fit or attractive as preferred. Minimal body intelligence, or somatic illiteracy, is a cultural norm as is an emphasis on logic, verbal abilities, and a trust in objective information. We know, for instance, how to cross the street but are unaware of whether we habitually step with the right foot or the left, sense our knee's misalignment to the pelvis, or feel the twinge of sadness in our belly. We may question and discount the value of such information. Yet the patterns of our responsiveness and expression impact our health and potential. Ignoring this vital information limits understanding not only who we are but also who we can become. When we take the time to sense, investigate, and reflect upon both obvious and subtle body events, which requires refining sensory understanding, we discover a rich amalgam of experiences.

The subjective information available through refining sensory experience is the area of somatics. The word *somatics* was coined in 1976 by Thomas Hanna, which he described as "the body as perceived from within."[5] The field, already the focus of pioneers like Charlotte Selver and Elsa Gindler (who developed Sensory Awareness), applies to exercises, philosophies, and methods of inquiry that support a subjective connection and sensitivity to one's personal body. Selver, Gindler, and other early practitioners paved the way for further practices and practitioners like Continuum (Emilie Conrad), Body-Mind Centering (Bonnie Bainbridge Cohen), and Dynamic Embodiment (Martha Eddy), among others. Such inquiries into bodily phenomena reveal habitual patterns of movement tied to posture, thought, and emotion and the deeper meaning that arises once we shine the light of awareness upon them. Senses awaken to new information, which impacts what and how we perceive, shifts that can have profound consequences with how we live with our body and with being itself.

HOW WE CONTINUE

The popping sensation in my belly mentioned in the introduction recalled the memory in the painter's studio. The two events reached across time to connect as if sequential despite years between them. Somehow they were related in the same way I sensed writing about them could influence the cataclysmic environmental, health, economic, and social challenges taking place across the United States and the globe, that it's important that we embrace all of who we are, a reckoning of the parts we greet with pride and the parts we avoid in shame, fear, or complacency. It's time to show up more fully, to grow up, heal, and connect beyond the provincial borders of a separate self and allow a shift in consciousness. Doing anything less is to shirk responsibility and violate oneself and others. Doing anything less means being complicit in the downfall of inhabitants upon this planet. We each can do our best by taking the available step before us. The specifics of that step are up to each one of us to determine, be it attending to the particulars of our body, writing a book, extending courtesy to a perceived Other, or changing how we consume goods. Historian Rebecca Solnit says, "Nobody can know the full consequences of their actions, and history is full of small acts that changed the world in surprising ways."[6]

My intention is to broaden minds to new ways of sensing, embodying, knowing, healing, opening, and innovating previously off-limits because cultural conventions ignored or belittled the steps leading there. It's heartbreaking to witness the steady extinction of plants and animals, extreme destructive storms, premature deaths, and polarized people hellbent on arguing their side to the point of dismissal and violence, their cheek turned away from common ground, empathy, and a broadened consciousness. We have entered a critical period in global history.

We can succumb to a poverty of imagination and empathy or rise above it. We can shutter our senses or cultivate their maturation.

This period is a pivot toward awakening to and embracing opportunities for developing new skills, increasing compassion for self and others, evolving beyond the limits of ego and cultural atrophy, and manifesting inherent potential. The time for action is now. That action involves greater acceptance and exploration of who we are, an acknowledgment of multiple perspectives, and awakening to our innate yet underutilized abilities.

My conclusion: We cannot operate as before. This can't continue.

I take that back. We could continue as before. But doing so implies an inability to accept dramatic and perilous changes already in process. To continue as before is a denial of the flow of life with the complexity of its interconnections. To continue as before is to be an accomplice to our demise and a refusal to grow up. Psychiatrist Elizabeth Kübler-Ross identified five stages encountered by a person facing terminal illness as denial, anger, bargaining, depression, and acceptance. Too many of us are in the early stages of her process: denial. Here's another perspective: Yes, we are facing a type of death, an existential crisis, but it's one of identity and consciousness similar to an adolescent crossing into adulthood. We're on the cusp of an evolutionary shift characterized by a change in habits and a more expansive awareness.

The better choice is awakening our senses, intuition, and intelligence to what is happening. A better choice is to gather available information and create new strategies to acknowledge our worries and make intelligent decisions. It's time to course correct and establish a balance that updates who we are, where we're headed, and who we can become.

The time is ripe for a great awakening and an expanded consciousness. The age of awakening is already happening. The disenfranchised are speaking out. People invested in racial and gender parity and environmental sustainability are actively working on solutions. Sources of toxicity are being identified and rooted out in favor of increased well-being and an enlivened and integrated spirit. Alternate forms of healing have entered the mainstream. Yoga and meditation are practiced by record numbers. We are questioning not only what we eat, but how it makes its way to our table. A 2018 report reveals that poverty has gone down by 40 percent worldwide for those suffering the worst.[7] It's up to each one of us to determine if we want to be part of the eroding order or the one that contains hope, healing, wholeness, and the way forward to a viable future. A beacon is shining upon previously dim areas of the mind.

2

An Integration of Energy Healing

The cell is a machine driven by energy. It can thus be approached by studying matter, or by studying energy. In every culture and in every medical tradition before ours, healing was accomplished by moving energy.

ALBERT SZENT-GYÖRGYI

As a preteen babysitting my brother a few years younger than me, I left the couch where we were watching TV to get a beverage. On my return I discovered him playing with a recently lit candle on the table, match in one hand, a finger of the other hand inserted into the flame like a small log. Were he older he would know how quickly flesh burns. I shouted for him to stop as the flame seared his flesh, his agonizing scream joining my fearful one in a chorus of terror.

Instinctively I grabbed his wrist and wrapped my hand around his sizzled finger. The hold was tight like a snug fitting glove as if to snuff the fire and pain. Then I yanked off the invisible glove and tossed it to the floor. He stopped crying.

"Does it hurt," I asked.

"No," he replied. He returned his gaze to the TV, his tears drying on his cheeks.

I did not mention the incident to our parents. It wasn't a matter of avoiding getting us into trouble. The episode resolved itself happily. There was no drama worth sharing, no burned flesh needing a doctor's visit, no fallout that required parental assistance. The incident seemed as mundane as stumbling on a rock or fallen branch in the woods behind our house. Reclaim balance, spy the culprit, take the next step, and do not give it a second thought.

Years pass. As a regular practitioner of Contact Improvisation, an improvisational dance that relies on following movement impulses and sharing weight and touch, I sat on the floor with my partner, our dance recently concluded. Often both partners move apart once the dance ends to find a new partner or retrieve a water bottle for a drink. Instead we stayed in place to chat while my hand, palm side down, draped on her shoulder, lingering longer than is customary, even among partners used to the extended touch that characterizes the dance. I felt moved to leave it there, my hand responding to her body's voiceless call to leave it in place, and she did not push it away. When I finally retracted my hand, she expressed astonishment.

"What were you doing? That was fantastic! I can't believe it!"

Unsure what had taken place, I asked for details.

"My neck pain is gone. My headache, too. What were you doing?" she replied.

Honestly I didn't know. I felt compelled to position my hand on her shoulder and rest it there. Somehow cued by an unstated invitation, my mind, which otherwise would have prompted me to retract my hand were we in a more public setting like a coffee shop, got out of the way. Over the years more incidents in the dance studio similarly compelled me to position my hand on a hip or back, followed by astonishment and a question about my method. My reply each time: "I don't know." My understanding went as far as following an impulse, a skill my improvisational dance training encouraged.

Improvisation invites playing with and stepping beyond common restrictions. It calls for spontaneity and responsiveness to sensory material free of analysis that can bog it down and impede flow and connection. Contact Improvisation, a primary dance practice of mine and topic of a previous book,* welcomes playing bodily with gravity, speed, space, weight, and motion with a fellow conspirator.

Calculated risks are encouraged but always with an eye toward respecting flexible boundaries and avoiding injury. Decades of dance in general and a daily meditation practice begun in my teens had cultivated heightened bodily sensitivity, a deep somatic listening, every moment fertile with possibility. Moving freely and sitting quietly reinforced developing an intimacy with the workings of my continually adapting body. They reinforced walking, studying, greeting friends and strangers, dreaming, and facing obstacles with ease, but at the time I had yet to understand the broader impact of these powerful activities.

My Don't Know replies led to suggestions that I pursue healing. Each time my well-meaning dance partner suggested the path, I said little, not even to ask a follow-up question. There were no healers in my family; my parents were owners of a small business. The term *healing* wasn't part of my upbringing or nomenclature. When I got sick, a doctor prescribed medicine to alleviate symptoms, injections for allergies, and physical therapy for structural challenges. When the worst of the symptoms disappeared, I was "better" and didn't question the method.

I translated comments about me becoming a healer as an expression of thanks, not a literal suggestion. Their comments briefly dangled in my mind until getting swept aside like so much chitchat. Their suggestion did not fit into my boxes, my filters classifying it as polite

---

*Contact Improvisation: An Introduction to a Vitalizing Dance Form. North Carolina: McFarland and Company, 2006.

nonsense, like when someone passing you in the hall says, "How are you?" and doesn't mean it as an opening to a conversation. I identified as a writer, dancer, and teacher. Those professional identities shaped my day-to-day affairs and consumed my attention. Those identities determined what took center stage and what did not get a seat in the theater. Such are the workings of a mind that each second must choose which of the myriad sensations, thoughts, memories, and feelings to allow into awareness, which to entertain or dismiss, choices made consciously and unconsciously.

A START OF HEALING

More years pass. I was living in South Korea and dancing in a *kut,* a healing ceremony that includes dance, this one orchestrated by the country's best-known shaman, Kim Keum-Hwa. The reason for my visit to her center was to write an article about her and investigate the transformative power of dance.*

I anticipated witnessing the ceremony and taking notes from the side of the room like an anthropologist operating on the principle of upholding objectivity and refraining from getting involved with the subject of her study. That principle quickly unraveled; I had not anticipated being invited to partake in the ritual by dancing. Saying no to a Korean, particularly an elder, is considered rude, so out of respect I accepted the invitation, accepted helpers dressing me in the customary white robe with oversized billowing sleeves, and welcomed dancing to the shrill flutes and insistent drums. As I witnessed others do, I bowed to Ms. Kim, her disciples, the musicians, and the altar loaded with fruit, sweet rice, and colorful papers. All received my bows before I kneeled, forehead to the floor in prostration. Returning upright, I

---

*The article "The Shamanic Heritage of a Korean Mudang" goes into the history of Korean shamanism and got published in *Shaman's Drum* 81 (2009).

hopped repeatedly, my gaze alternately down and forward, my arms extended up and outward. The dance lasted long enough for me to straddle foreign gestures with familiar moves, spins, undulations, outward extensions, and contractions, then slowing to step forward and sideways. When my dancing ended and I returned to my seat, Ms. Kim invited me to join her table for lunch, our chopsticks clutching a feast of rice, seaweed, mackerel, lotus root, and other foods from a grid of bowls. It's then she told me about my healing ability and urged me to pursue a path as a healer.

Again. Another person echoing a suggestion like those of my dance partners, except this time, I couldn't dismiss it as small talk. Sometimes hearing the same idea twice, or in my case multiple times, erodes mental walls, the filters slip off, and closed doors crack open. Hearing it from a North Korean–born war survivor, whose past contains heartache and bloodshed and whose homeland includes centuries of indigenous healing rites, carried substantive gravity. It took up residence in my mind like a puzzle piece fallen to the floor compelling me to lean down to retrieve it and examine the emerging patterns until finding its rightful place in the picture.

On moving back to the United States, I explored which of the many healing modalities to study. My body would tire from the muscular exertion of massage, so I ruled out a physically taxing technique like Swedish massage or Rolfing. I considered acupuncture for its impressive volume of knowledge of the body's energy meridians but inserting stainless steel needles into the skin lacked my preference for sensual, embodied connection. The meditative calm and gentle touches of energy healing held appeal. More than that, though, its practice intrigued me. How could hands hovering near or resting upon the surface of a body activate healing? How could my hands hundreds of miles from a client perform a distant healing? What is this energy, also referred to (depending on the culture) as subtle energy, universal energy, chi, ki, or prana?

Practicality landed me at studying Reiki because a nearby licensed professional counselor was offering classes. I sat in those first meetings eager to ask questions. I wanted to know, for instance, about the use of my boyfriend's newest phone, an iPhone he boasted as superior to my flip version. A few seconds of my fingers tapping and swiping the screen burned my fingertips. "How is this usable?" I complained with Luddite irreverence, preferring the superiority of my phone before dropping his onto his lap.

"You feel no heat?" I asked in disbelief. "Nothing?" I pressed, demonstrating my swipe motion in case the burn resulted from improper finger placement.

"Nothing," he replied firmly as our divergent experiences eyed each other with suspicion, a perceptual gap that challenged each other's version of truth.

The Reiki training period marked the return of electrical mayhem in my house. My flipping a light switch blew the bulb in the living room, then a ceiling light in the hallway, then a table lamp, my touch setting off small room-to-room explosions. Battery-operated clocks in the bedroom and office also in the line of fire stopped working and required replacement batteries. An electrician investigating the wiring found no problem in the walls or the central box in the basement.

Sharing my combustive tale lit up the faces of fellow students without the anticipated laughter and grimaces. "The same thing happened to me with my bedroom lamp," said the woman beside me as she recalled a similar tale of electrical currents gone awry. "My kitchen light," said another.

"It's common," said my teacher, grinning, before she explained how to ground the body's energy and send Reiki to our electronic gadgets. Until this point I had not considered healing anything other than humans though was open to applying it to cats, dogs, and horses, but sending Reiki to a phone challenged my notion of our relationships with inanimate devices of utility, despite their pivotal role in a modern home. Would my toaster oven and electric pencil sharpener be next? After grounding myself with feet firmly on the floor, I set the phone on the table and placed my dubious hands around its aluminum alloy surface. Neither of us gave off sparks or spontaneously combusted, an imagining likely the result of watching one too many Hollywood movies. Since sharing my circuitry with the hidden wires of my boyfriend's phone and the iPhone I soon purchased for myself, the only heat they now generate comes from animated conversations with tech support about my frustration with malfunctioning hardware on my computer. My destructive force with bulbs and batteries has gladly been decommissioned and stored safely as a memory.

THE POWER OF TOUCH

A more pleasant sensation occurred through human touch. When my teacher placed her hands on my shoulders and waved them around my head and torso to carry out a Reiki Attunement, an initiation ritual that opens a body to energetic healing pathways for use with oneself and others, it was as if she accessed a secret faucet. The motion released an energizing and soothing warm stream that coursed throughout my body. It began at my head and flowed down my neck into my shoulders, traveling to my belly, legs, and feet. My awareness then shifted to the space beyond my skin similarly filling with this current. Even with her hands lifted off my body, I continued to feel their every position as if her fingers extended beyond their tips and the sensitive surface of my skin extended beyond its dermal layer, the fabric of my body elasticizing and losing its solidity. The experience reminded me of times on the dance floor when a lengthy muscular exertion and deepened breath led to the space around me feeling lighter, as if the air thinned from a higher altitude or lower humidity, and I was moving with uncharacteristic and unanticipated effortlessness. I was reminded, too, of writing in flow, each word journeying easily from mind to page in the splash of a moment. Deliriously sobering, grounding, and otherworldly, Reiki energy behaved as close kin to generative creative energy, which, when engaged, when my attention turns toward its flux, invites me into the home of my body and the interconnectivity of being.

Upon receiving my certification as a Reiki practitioner, the teacher encouraged me to hang my shingle. I didn't. The assessment of my abilities left me feeling ill prepared and uncomfortable about inviting a client onto a massage table for treatment. Invite someone onto the dance floor—sure. Create a narrative—certainly. Years of dancing, writing, and teaching hadn't yet made room for believing in my curative ability, so I pursued additional training in Healing Touch. This three-year program involved working alongside nurses, doctors, and healers trained in a variety of modalities and engaging in conversations about the bands of energy that surround and infiltrate the body, revealing our skin as a semipermeable boundary intimately tied to individual and collective health. Several hundred sessions of working on clients with depression, anxiety, migraines, chronic pain, cancer, concussions, PTSD, and a host of other ailments have taught me how the body manifests unease and disease, my hands and energetic sensitivity acting as informative conduits.

Previously my hands were known to hold pens and tap away at keyboards. They have clutched hammers and forks, flipped switches, unlocked car doors, lifted the hair from my eyes, pushed against the floor to roll with a dance partner, and grazed a lover's body, but in healing my hands entered new territory and their intelligence increased tenfold. With an aim to support and restore health, they have learned how to slip into and dance in the shadows of a body and settle upon skin and clothing to uncover the secrets and marvels of the flesh. They feel heat and cool, density and brightness, anger and fear, pulse and dart. They penetrate surfaces without injury, disfiguring, or surgical intrusion. These sensitive tactile detectors and transmitters reveal a level of reality not perceived by my eyes. The literacy of my hands picks up on this universal flow, what scientists at the National Institutes of Health call the *biofield*. Quantum physics defines it as an electromagnetic field generated by the body's biological processes, that such a field is based on "electromagnetic fields, coherent states, biophotons, quantum and quantum-like processes."[1] Biophysics researcher James Oschman recognizes our sensory systems as vibration detectors, vibration being a pivotal characteristic of the energies around us. He says there is "no single 'life force' or 'healing energy.' Instead, there are many systems in the body that store, release, conduct, and utilize various kinds of energy and information."[2] Energy healer Cyndi Dale describes it as "the pure and free-flowing energy that activates and nurtures life and connects the small and the great."[3] This substance is difficult to measure with current technology and, like atoms and cells, is imperceptible with any of the five senses. What does this suggest about bodies that most of us understand as solid, physical matter?

Time to open the mind, to quiet its tendency to quick judgment. Time to allow the senses to roam beyond their usual confines. Time to welcome an influx of information without relying on the usual channels.

Sensing this life energy requires expanding our perceptive range and becoming quiet, still, and impartial to be receptive to the activity that dwells just outside common perception. It requires shifting our attention to what we may have previously ignored because we were elsewhere preoccupied. It requires us to unplug our usual biases and filters that lock us in place. It requires us to relax into open attention and receptivity. It requires us to wonder, trust, and practice. Whether we want relief from suffering for ourselves or another, we let go of the ego's clutches and put our agenda aside to avail ourselves of a current connected to something larger than the limits of our thinking and singular effort. Sensing and working with the biofield requires sidestepping usual distractions and welcoming a healing presence that at any given moment is interpersonal, transpersonal, and transcendent. It is meditation in motion, touch amplified, and entry into a dream that cuts through

falsehoods and common story lines. It is a return to a primordial awareness, indigenous knowledge, and innate intelligence.

SUBTLE ENERGY

This universal energy is the core ingredient of Reiki, which is both a
healing modality and a philosophy about cultivating peace, harmony,
and health, suggested ideals that most healing practitioners readily welcome. Reiki derives from two Japanese words, *rei,* which means "god's
wisdom or higher power," and *ki,* which means "life force energy." Reiki
began in the late 1800s in Japan with Mikao Usui. Although details
of his life are disputed, it is generally thought Usui studied various
forms of Japanese martial arts, Christian and Buddhist theology, and
healing traditions from several cultures. While practicing meditation
at a Japanese monastery, he received a vision with symbols intended
to establish a practitioner's intention for use at the start and close of a
healing session, along with a combination of hands-on and hands-off
techniques. Initially he applied the work to his family and himself, but
a move to Tokyo that coincided with the Great Kanto earthquake and
tsunami in 1923 led him to share and develop his technique with more
of the population. To help spread the use of Reiki, Usui performed
numerous attunements and led trainings.*

Healing Touch began in the United States with Janet Mentgen in
the 1980s and developed over the next few decades while she worked
as a nurse treating patients in the U.S. Navy, in emergency rooms, and
in home health care. She questioned whether the laying on of hands, a
practice associated with priests invoking the Holy Spirit during bap-
tisms and healing, required religious belief. Not religious herself, she

---

*For more on the origins of Reiki see Diane Stein's *Essential Reiki: A Complete Guide
to an Ancient Healing Art* (Freedom, Calif.: The Crossing Press, 1995) and William
Lee Rand's article "What Is the History of Reiki," which can be found on his website
under FAQs.

experimented with her patients and found their speed of recovery was faster and more effective than those who received no Healing Touch. She shared her findings with fellow nurses and doctors and eventually established a program to train practitioners, which was especially suited for use in hospitals and health care settings.*

Many of my clients come to me after a more conventional route yields little or no improvement in their condition. Elena came for treatment of her chronic ankle pain. She fractured it during a skiing mishap a year earlier. Her doctor explained that the fracture would be healed after a few months and she would be able to stand and walk pain free. The few months passed with no alleviation of the pain. The doctor told her she was exaggerating her symptoms and sent her away. As I worked on Elena's ankle, I felt excessive heat pouring out from the site of the fracture. I placed my hands gently around her ankle, then raked my fingers through the area beyond her skin until the heat cooled and matched the temperature of the rest of her body. Upon getting off the table and walking around the room, she reported the pain gone, and when I checked up on her months later, she reported that it had not returned.

Jean came to me complaining about chronic debilitating migraines that wiped her out for days and disrupted her ability to focus on getting anything done. As my hands moved around her body, I felt a protrusion extending several inches from her head in the shape of a spike. If my hands passed through it, she flinched with pain so I found its outermost point and cupped my hands around it without moving to soften the point. Careful not to do any sudden motion that provoked another flinch, I slowly reduced the length of the spike as if erasing it, eventually dissolving it altogether. When my hands further

---

*For more on the origins of Healing Touch see Diane Wind Wardell's *White Shadow: Walking with Janet Mentgen* (Lakewood, Colo.: Colorado Center for Healing Touch, 2000). Much of my knowledge on the origins of Healing Touch also came from a 2013 lecture with Deborah Larrimore, a student of Janet Mentgen's.

investigated the area around her body, they encountered floating jagged clusters as if a debris field from a plane crash. I cleared these away as if sweeping a floor of metal shards crusted over by clumps of dirt. When I mentioned the shards later, she told me that she was shot by an ex-boyfriend a decade ago and doctors were unable to remove all the shrapnel from her body.

The sensitivity of my hands has revealed the shape and feel of various ailments. Concussions feel like a lopsided quivery balloon jutting out from a side of the skull. Infections feel clammy and dark. Cancer feels hot and electric. Anger comes across as sharp tingles. Obsessive thinking and anxiety is a chaotic tangle of ricocheting threads and particles. The field of someone on the autistic spectrum feels metallic, extends out atypically far, and is highly sensitive to motion, which has prompted me to work several feet away. It is immensely gratifying to watch clients get off the massage table, where the majority of the work takes place, their suffering reduced or gone.

The practice of my hands leads to expanding my understanding of touch. Touch is frequently framed as a subject performing action upon an object—I touch Jean. It's the common parlance and grammar. The I assumes the active role as subject with an action, touch, played out upon a passive recipient, the object, Jean in this example. The grammatical order skews our thinking and reinforces an egocentric perspective. We experience ourselves as the star of our drama, the central figure from which all events take place. We must be reminded—a slight stretch—that the object of our touch is also a subject, that Jean is also touching me, a lovely role reversal. She is as much a central figure as I am. Our bodies make contact, our energy fields overlap, and we both maintain a center. If anything, the two-way street of touch makes us bicentric, or polycentric if there are more than two people. It positions us in a mutual encounter, a meeting between bodies sensing each other with available skills.

For those who are attentive, my touching you provides information about you and the touch also provides you with information about me.

The place of contact opens the gate to all sorts of information, especially for healers whose highly sensitive hands rest gently on the skin surface and in the subtle field of the body to detect heat, cool, tingles, pressure, and more. This mutual relationship of connection increases awareness. Says phenomenologist Maurice Merleau-Ponty referring to touch in general, "[M]y body simultaneously sees and is seen. . . . It sees itself seeing; it touches itself touching; it is visible and sensitive for itself. . . . Visible and mobile, my body is a thing among things; it is caught in the fabric of the world."[4] Touch establishes an organic bond between us through the largest organ of the body, the skin, with its complex network of neural pathways and more than a million sensory receptors in the connective tissue of the subcutaneous hypodermis, the dermis, and the topmost layer, the epidermis. It's no wonder that so many of us get so touchy about the people who brush up against us accidentally or intentionally; one brief encounter can open the gates to an onslaught of sensations. Sharing a caring touch reduces stress and provokes the release of oxytocin, which enhances our emotional and physical well-being. No wonder, too, that touch deprivation leads to a sense of isolation and a weakened immune system.

Every part of the body leads to a specific awareness, emotion, sensation, imagery, and/or memory, perceptible to those who notice. Movement therapist and founder of Body-Mind Centering, Bonnie Bainbridge Cohen, refers to the different systems of the body, the organs, glands, muscles, bones, fluids, and nervous system as "minds." She recognizes the development of a preverbal awareness based on touch and movement. When working on someone, she says, "I will go into that area of my own body to see. In the process I become more open also. It becomes like two bells ringing on the same pitch. We can resonate each other."[5]

With an intent to heal, my hands enter the space or touch the surface of another's body, the palms potent conductors of healing biofield energy, but it's not like the rest of me stays behind on the couch to flip through a magazine. My hands are connected to arms, a torso, a head, mind, intention, and awareness, and where my hands and intention go, the rest of me goes, too. We are not engaging in casual conversation nor discussing the stock market. Usual filters quiet and are suspended to make way for a silent transpersonal exchange that takes place on a potent, subtle, bodily level. The connection is unmediated, direct, felt, and visceral, an assertion of personal experience that contributes to individual embodiment and wholeness.

We typically think of touch as a skin to skin, body to body encounter, our solid physical self meeting the solidity of another, but touch begins much sooner. Many of us are familiar with feeling someone eyeing us, even from the opposite side of the room with our back to them. This is an example of the sense receptors of the skin at work, the beam of eyes felt like a graze. A heightened sense ability is a latent skill that anyone can develop through practice. My Reiki and Healing Touch training transformed my chance sensitivity that led to helping my dance partners into an ability deliberately accessed for many more people. It was a matter of switching attention, developing a new type of focus, and practicing. Many of my university students taking Contact Improvisation report it helping with concentration. Football players in my classes have used their newly acquired awareness of the biofield to sharpen their peripheral awareness and agility on the athletic field during games and report improved performance, among the reasons that so many sign up for the class each semester.

My tactile sense is well developed, influenced by decades of dance, which has increased my kinesthetic and proprioceptive sensitivity, every nuance packed with information that is potentially useful. Dancers are continually fine-tuning the instrument of their body, their muscle, breath, focus, and timing, carrying out complex movements that sync up with fellow dancers. But unrelated to dance training, my visual and auditory senses have developed, too. I see images and hear voices but not in the usual way of relying on light entering my cornea or sound waves vibrating my cochlea. Such was the case with Dana, who came to me with depression. As I neared the end of our healing session, the image of a woman appeared. Initially I questioned the vision as a fiction of my imagination before I turned my attention toward the wraithlike presence. In her seventies, she stood near the table in a colorful, loosely fitted, matronly dress. She looked at my client, then me, and said, "Please tell her not to repeat my mistakes." Then she was gone.

In receiving inexplicable visions such as this, I must decide whether sharing the information is beneficial to the client or if their filters will discount the information or judge me as off the wall. I determined the former given the woman's profession as a therapist and my assumption of her understanding of imagination as a storehouse for unconscious and nascent material. "I don't know who this woman is but . . . " My client teared up. She recognized the woman as her mother with whom she had a difficult life-long relationship. Dana had replicated the pattern with her own daughter who was due to visit the following day. Dana received her mother's comment as a recognition of their painful relationship and an attempt at forgiveness. The advice was timely and welcome and prompted more tears about her pattern of pain, which our session motivated her not to perpetuate.

Honestly, had this vision taken place years earlier, there's a good chance of me judging it as too woo-woo and ignoring it. I take pride in being reasonable, balanced, and dismissive of superstition. I have walked beneath ladders and lived with a black cat who has regularly curled up on my lap without unleashing any sort of mayhem other than covering my pants with fur. But pride or any other ideal held too tightly is a type of blinder that conceals other truths. Ignoring my experience would have meant withholding a pivotal element for Dana's healing process. Energy healing, much like meditation, positions me in a twilight of consciousness, a liminal space that is neither here nor there, a quality of presence that suspends common filters. Here the doors of perception open, the nervous system quiets, brain waves shift, and habit patterns that determine attention and action are suspended temporarily to make way for new experiences.

EXPANDED PERCEPTIONS AS PART OF HEALING

Visions such as the one with Dana's mother place many of us at an edge of comfort, credibility, and understanding. The world as we know it gives way. The limits of our consciousness buckle. It's the As Yet to Be Understood, what we may perceive as not fitting into our belief system. It's also the very territory that needs more attention and study. I'm going to repeat the last sentence because of its importance to our development: it's also the very territory that needs more attention and study. Many of us are weak in somatic literacy, the ability to notice our sensory phenomenon and understand its meaning. Additionally, most of us are perceptual adolescents who are untrained—perhaps lazy, unwilling, or ill-equipped—to step beyond cultural conditioning. As a result, we access only a fraction of the billions of neurons of our brain. What else is possible when we open the doors and turn attention away from our usual patterns of perceiving? What abilities and gifts have we overlooked? It would seem that a skilled mind should be less interested in experiences that reinforce what is already known in favor of discovering a type of attention and information that aligns with larger truths. Advancing this type of skill seems especially critical now with so many of our systems falling short of sustaining health and well-being, the foundation of so many institutions showing significant cracks, the Earth itself delivering more and more variable and extreme weather.

Phenomena such as visions can be reframed as a call to expand a perception, an intuition pointing away from the usual direction or habits of our mind, a sign that leads to new abilities. Its unconventional path is similar to how artists, inventors, entrepreneurs, and others come upon fresh material. They follow their gut, an impulse, a dream, a question, an inspiration, or an oddity that catches their attention. Here lies a frontier of consciousness beckoning exploration. Here lies perceptual muscles in need of flexing. Here lies an undeveloped ability and intelligence, the universe trying to shake us awake. Marginalizing such abilities prevents us from reaping its benefits and clips potential. Avoiding such abilities minimizes our experience of wholeness.

Pursuing expanded perceptions can deliver previously unimagined goods and may contain the very ingredients not only to our survival but also to our thriving. If we're willing to open. If we're willing to look. If we relax our rush to judgment and suspend our usual constructs for framing knowing. If we're curious.

These anomalous experiences can also be understood through the frame of imagination. A function of the mind, imagination is the mechanism that loosens ego and mental constructs for nimbly climbing or leaping to a new perspective. Imagination is calisthenics for the senses and the wings that let us fly above them. It is the great initiator birthing new ideas and understanding. Imagination is like the stepping stones that allow us to cross unnavigable waters. It is the pair of hands available when others are tied up.

Sometimes I intentionally engage a client's imagination to aid their healing, essentially collaborating in the dream and symbolic experience of their body. This approach has proven especially helpful with those struggling with trauma, chronic pain, and other intransigent conditions. Sometimes the body can welcome a symbol better than a more direct query. It reframes the unconscious and disowned experiences as less threatening. Hal had survived years of physical, emotional, and verbal abuse from his mother and coped early on through dissociation. Through years of psychotherapy, medication, acupuncture, and a host of other treatments, he managed to marry, raise a family, and become an executive-level manager, able to compartmentalize these areas from his early suffering. He came to me with depression, an inability to feel emotions, and a need to "lift the pressure off his chest" that restricted his breathing, a symptom that baffled his pulmonologist who claimed there was nothing wrong with him.

The metaphor of "lifting pressure" describing his condition was my entry. After first calming his nervous system and getting his permission to collaborate imaginally, I gently placed my hands on the site of the pressure and asked for further information. Immediately his difficulty breathing increased.

"There's something around my throat," he said. "I think it's a hand."

My fingertips gently grazed his throat to reinforce a somatic connection to keep him present with me and the dream while also being careful to avoid retraumatizing him. "Can I unlatch it, untie it, or cut it off?"

"No," he said. "Pull it off."

To reinforce his calm, I verbalized what I would do with his assistance and proceeded only upon his approval. "I'm placing my hands beneath it now. It's a bit difficult to grab. Can you lift your chin? Oh, I think I have it. Yes, I've a firm grasp." Meanwhile I'm miming the actions just above his body and lightly stroking his neck. "Okay, on the count of three," I said, successfully removing it before returning to his sternum.

I encouraged him to imagine the pressure at his chest. "Is something binding your torso? Is it a liquid pressure?" I asked, an intuitive hit that brought up a memory of his mom trying to drown him in a bathtub. "Would it be better if I helped you out of the tub or let the water drain?"

"Drain," he replied firmly. As the water ran out, I spoke about details like watching the water level lower, his bent knees and other parts of his body emerging above the water, and the air around him feeling more cool and less moist. I then helped him to his feet, gave him a towel, and opened the window so he could look out and see the sun and feel its warmth. By the conclusion of the session, he shed a few tears, reported the pressure was gone, and he was breathing deeper than he knew was possible.

WHAT IS HEALING?

Healing is now part of my nomenclature. The word *heal* comes from the Old English "haelen" with a Greek origin, "holos." A prime definition of healing according to *Merriam-Webster Dictionary* is "to make sound or whole." Healing considers one's entire well-being and recognizes the confluence of one's physical, emotional, mental, spiritual, and energetic self. Healing is an active process that includes investigating our attitudes, memories, beliefs, and relationships. It includes releasing any negative patterns that play a role in preventing a full recovery and is an unconditional embrace of who we are. To be whole, that is, undamaged, unhurt, and safe, is directly tied to health and being healed.

Healing differs from curing, which is typically the focus of traditional Western medicine that strives to eradicate symptoms. Typically a cure originates from someone other than us, like a doctor. Curing aims to remove evidence of disease, the disappearance of symptoms a godsend for the sufferer. A cure does not consider an underlying cause, which can mean the illness modifies and new symptoms appear later. Nor does it take into account associated emotional and psychological stressors. For example, if a stressful workload at the office leads to high blood pressure, taking a pill to relax blood vessels will only go so far. With the cause not addressed, the ignored stressor may manifest later as shoulder pain, irritability, or depression. Additionally, the process leading to a cure is passive, the patient giving over authority to the physician and prescribed treatment.

Western medicine, also referred to as traditional or allopathic medicine, is effective in identifying problems, prescribing medication, and performing surgeries. Tied to science and technology, traditional medicine can be a best friend to those with a life-threatening disease, a broken bone, ruptured organs, or a virulent virus. Among its strengths, traditional medicine is able to zero in on a specific part of the body, the symptom needing attention, and address the problem through a potent, targeted treatment. Doctors can perform modern miracles such as identifying and altering problematic genes, inserting a pacemaker into a chest with a sluggish heart, and prescribing antibiotics and other medicines. To the sufferer, the know-how of traditional medicine can be the difference between life and death.

Reiki and Healing Touch are part of a broader field also referred to as energy healing, energy medicine, complementary medicine, alternative medicine, and integrative medicine. Of the various terms, *alternative medicine* does energy healing the greatest disservice. *Alternative* suggests moving ahead with one *or* another treatment, for instance undergoing surgery for lung cancer *or* receiving energy healing. There are exceptions, but typically one should not consider one treatment in lieu of another. In most instances pursuing both treatments is advisable, the strength of the approaches working together in partnership. Surgery removes the cancerous tumor and energy healing hastens the restoration of the health of the tissue, boosts the immune system, and minimizes or eradicates the need for pain medication. Studies of Healing Touch show that energy medicine reduces and eliminates cancer cells without surgery or chemotherapy but relying solely on energy healing at the start should depend on the stage of the cancer and how well a patient responds to energy treatments.[6]

Complementary medicine is a more helpful term. It emphasizes that a technique works in conjunction with a traditional allopathic treatment. Another helpful term is *integrative,* which suggests the importance of a comprehensive plan. According to Duke Integrative Medicine, *integrative medicine* is considered an approach "to care that puts the patient at the center and addresses the full range of physical, emotional, mental, social, spiritual and environmental influences that affect a person's health" using "a personalized strategy that considers the patient's unique conditions, needs and circumstances."[7] A care team in integrative medicine may recommend surgery while also looking at nutrition, family relationships, self-care activities, energy healing, and mindfulness practices.

Integrative health involves a variety of factors: stress, food, exercise, sleep, thoughts, memories, work, relationships, sex, and environment. Any one of these categories can be broken down further to include areas such as dreams, creative activity, vacations, affirmations, empathy, and sustainability. Among other factors, integrative health involves identifying cultural influences that may have negative and positive impacts. For instance, living beneath a busy eight-lane highway and working for a demanding boss has a different effect than living on a hillside beside an alpine grove and being part of a supportive team. Determining what area needs to be emphasized to restore and maintain balance depends upon what's out of whack and where we're situated on the continuum of health.

Despite its many benefits, traditional medicine has significant faults. One fault is its close ties to the pharmaceutical industry, which leads to doctors overprescribing medicine, some with side effects so detrimental as to offset the positives. The opioid epidemic, which has generated widespread addiction and death, is one such tragic example. An adverse effect of some antidepressants is insomnia, which interferes with one's ability to function during the day and often requires an additional pill to bring on sleep. A second fault is the exorbitant expense of treatments that insurance companies and politicians seem uninterested in reining in, contributing to the United States having the highest costs for health care among developed nations.[8] Inadequate responses and inaction by the health care industry controlled by a profit model results in patients seeking financial help through crowdfunding sites such as GoFundMe, going bankrupt, forfeiting treatment (which can have fatal results), or participating in medical tourism. In 2016, eleven million Americans traveled outside the country to places like Mexico,

South Korea, and Thailand for treatment, saving as much as 80 percent of their health care costs.[9] That the U.S. health care system is bloated, inadequate except for the wealthy, and in need of an overhaul is the topic for another book and another author. Lastly, an additional fault— also a strength—of traditional medicine is its focus on a body part and symptom while neglecting the involvement of the entirety of the body.

Energy healing, which includes modalities such as polarity therapy, craniosacral therapy, Therapeutic Touch, and pranic healing, among others, goes by names such as energy therapy, energy medicine, subtle energy medicine, vibrational medicine, spiritual healing, laying on of hands, and the preferred term of the NIH, *biofield therapy*. Oschman regards energy healing as an "energy of a particular frequency or set of frequencies that stimulates the repair of one or more tissues. The cascade of activities initiated by such signals may provide essential information to cells and tissues, and open channels for the flow of information that coordinates repair processes."[10] These repairs can improve the functioning of the neurological, cardiovascular, respiratory, skeletal, and endocrinal systems. At its core is restoring and maintaining the flow of biofield energy, or universal energy, within and beyond the body responsible for equilibrium. Its effectiveness in treating ailments has captured the attention of more and more researchers, including those at the NIH, who see it as the next wave in medicine. Its popularity trails behind Eastern medicine practices like acupuncture, whose practitioners long ago recognized the pervasiveness of chi and tapped into centuries worth of knowledge for dealing with a variety of health issues.

Energy medicine's acceptance in the West has been slowed by a lack of equipment that accurately measures energy. The West relies on and favors objective, evidence-based knowledge over subjective methods despite both providing useful information. The bias against subjective knowledge, among other reasons, results in researchers playing catch-up in understanding how biofield therapies work. One of energy medicine's ardent supporters is Richard Gerber, a researcher and doctor of internal medicine who says, "Our subtle-energy bodies play a major role in maintaining our health. Energy disturbances in the etheric body precede the manifestation of abnormal patterns of cellular organization and growth."[11] Another supporter is research psychologist Gary Schwartz, who conducted numerous experiments, "witnessed too many healings . . . and personally experienced too many healings myself as a patient. . . . At some point, there comes a time when the evidence is too great to be ignored."[12]

OPTIMAL HEALTH

Health is a balance of the ongoing dynamic of the many parts of us. Optimal health brings us close to our true self and fulfillment of our potential. At our best, we are pain-free and vibrant. We feel at home with our body and fellow bodies. We experience our body as remarkable, mysterious, and *salutogenic,* a term coined by medical sociologist Aaron Antonovsky that refers to our natural tendency to move toward health. Much like the positive psychology movement's focus on wellness versus traditional psychology's focus on illness, we welcome practices that support health and well-being. Holistic nurse and author Barbara Dossey says, "Healing is the emergent process of the whole system bringing together aspects of one's self and the components of body–mind–spirit–culture–environment at deeper levels of inner knowing. This leads to integration and balance, and each aspect has equal importance and value."[13]

The power of subtle energy (the biofield) for healing continually amazes me. I am grateful to be able to harness it for the health and well-being of others. Every sufferer wants to feel better, and it's hard to witness anyone coming up short. It's helpful, however, to recognize betterment as a continuum that depends on the conditions of our mental, physical, emotional, energetic, and spiritual needs. Abraham Maslow's Hierarchy of Needs is a good reminder that what preoccupies us at any given moment depends upon needs he classifies into three categories: basic, which includes safety and the physiological need for food, water, warmth, and rest; psychological, which includes a sense of belonging, love and self-esteem; and self-fulfillment, which includes activities that contribute to self-actualization and fulfilling our highest potential. One typically does not move up the hierarchy until the needs of one level are satisfied. For instance, a person in chronic pain (basic) may have no interest in throwing a party (sense of belonging) or want to take up meditation (self-fulfillment) for the purpose of reaching higher states of consciousness until pain levels decrease.

Below is a sample of several markers on the betterment list to determine where you are on the continuum:

in pain	pain-free
worried	calm
tired	energized
depressed & unmotivated	excited & engaged
denying	accepting
alienated	sense of belonging
unaware & reactive	aware & responsive
judgmental	compassionate
egotistical	altruistic
anthropocentric	eco- or cosmocentric
locked into a singular perspective	cognizant of multiple perspectives

Being at any one of these places is not inherently good or bad. Critical steps in any healing process mean accepting where one is, feeling gratitude despite difficulty, and using our situation as an opportunity to alter habits and grow. Of course, pain is, well, painful, even debilitating, and can lead to lashing out at our body or another unfortunate target who happens to be nearby. Yet recognizing what is taking place bodily and noticing the sensorimotor, proprioceptive, and energetic phenomena is useful information. If approached with gentleness and curiosity, pain can lead to greater self-knowing and peace. It becomes the very path to growth. If we're up to it, which I strongly encourage, it's a worthwhile door to unlock, step through, and look around.

Too often, we wish reality to be other than it is, or we remain oblivious to our body's signals, which indicates a low degree of somatic literacy. Somatic literacy, which for most of us remains undeveloped, supports us detecting and interpreting our body's many signals. There is great power in acknowledging the present moment with all its messy, fleeting, puzzling, unsettling, painful, contradictory, and astonishing phenomena. Too often, we resist What Is and find respite in excuses, victimization, or a story about reality whose usefulness has passed. For instance, my client Mary attributed her father's abuse as cause for her depression. Her awareness is helpful in understanding and facing the cause, but harmful when the story impedes emotional and energetic growth, when her understanding and self-compassion don't evolve and get in the way of adopting new behaviors that reinforce her strengths. It's important to regularly touch into the active stream of sensation, perceptions, subtle energy, and renewal taking place every moment. This awareness accesses all of who we are and does not lock us into a restrictive narrative.

Ironically, resistance to What Is reinforces that which we're resisting. It reinforces an argument with the evidence before us. Resistance perpetuates the existence of the very condition we'd rather not experience. "I shouldn't be feeling this way," complain many of my clients. Or "It's not who I am." None of us are our pain, but pain may be the condition of our body at that moment, and we would be wise to listen and attend to its message. Better to give ourselves compassion. Better to connect bodily and acknowledge the sensations involved with What Is to open the door to relief and growth. Better to acknowledge present details and use them to make informed decisions. Better to investigate the contents of our thoughts.

Accepting What Is may seem great if we are mildly tired and not so great if we're suffering from the debilitating effects of fibromyalgia or despairing about being unemployed. Acceptance does not mean solidifying the present and its conditions. It's not a giving up. If anything, it's an acceptance of changing conditions. The body changes. Circumstances change. Feelings and thoughts change. New information emerges all the time. Change is constant, is indeed the only constant. Accepting What Is contributes to ease and supports changes rooted in an informed, personalized relationship with our body. Our subtle energy flows, every bodily system supported in fulfilling its function to the best of its ability. Listening to and tending deeply to our body allows its wisdom to emerge. It reveals the path to its own betterment and integrative well-being. Acceptance of What Is is a necessary step in our recovery. Acceptance of What Is can liberate us from our suffering and is the very path underfoot.

Easy to write about, but harder to do. Which is why mindful, embodied practices and guidance from a professional help. To differentiate sound from noise, an image from a blur, a clear signal from static. To know what is helpful and what is detrimental. To know when we're off track and when we're on. To know what uplifts us and what brings us down. To point out which filters get in the way and which lead the way. To feel the levity of encouragement when discouragement weighs us down.

My health is incomplete without a regular movement practice in my home, the dance studio, or a park. Sometimes what is craved is the airing out and centering that accompanies the blood and oxygen rush from repeated forceful movements. Frequently, it's the slightest motion or deepening of a stretch warming my heart, activating energy centers, and lubricating the connective tissue toward opening awareness. It may appear that my head or torso have tilted, or my hand has lifted—all part of it—but it's also the energy of my biofield shifting that prompts a deepening of breath and sensory sensitivity. The shift provokes a subtle yet profound alteration to consciousness, my sensory awareness heightened. My previous self loosens its fixity as I press into the floor, expand ribs, and clear bodily channels in a dance with being. The pattern of activity of the previous hour or days is given an opportunity for renewal through expression. Deliberately I engage with flow.

Dance ranks among my most potent of medicines with ample beneficial side effects and allows me to inhabit the full breadth of my body. Writing has a similar effect, especially when it coincides with a somatic and energetic awareness to alchemize body, breath, and matter, taking me into the frontier of new possibility. Somatically and energetically based writing typically ushers in insights, visions, and a vibrant resonance that provides immediate satisfaction, every word on the page essential to a pattern emerging, regardless of level of craft. Details about who I am rise up, a looking within that coincides with seeing outside me. Every word matters, every breath, every seeing and feeling, and somehow amid the swirl of details, I settle into a peace like the pleasure of walking a wooded path.

THE OPPORTUNITY IN UNEASE AND DISEASE

Although I wouldn't wish difficulties on anyone, illness and unease are rich opportunities for growth—if we choose to embrace them as such. It's not its purpose or *raison d'être,* which is an oversimplification of multiple causes and conditions, but illness provides useful information toward positive ends. Our ailment is the body's way of getting our attention about an imbalance. Stress, tension, inflammation, flu, anxiety, cancer, or any other condition may be our body's way of asking us to slow down, to eat less sugar, to sleep more, to forgive, to walk in the park, to take up drawing, to join a religious community, or to increase consciousness. Essentially, the body is communicating that something is out of whack and a behavior or attitude needs modification. This applies as well to dire circumstances that are outside our control. Says psychologist and holocaust survivor Viktor Frankl, "The way in which a man accepts his fate and all the suffering it entails, the way in which he takes up his cross, gives him ample opportunity—even under the most difficult circumstances—to add a deeper meaning to his life."[14] The rupture of the norm provides an opportunity to reconfigure balance and stir abilities that may have been dormant. Our current social, environmental, economic, and health upheavals are providing an epic opportunity toward establishing a better way of life.

The Chinese word for crisis is composed of two characters, one representing danger and the other representing opportunity. In crisis is opportunity, that is, when we take the time to investigate, when we tend to ourselves with curiosity, when we choose to use the circumstance to our benefit and not solely wish for its disappearance. Encouraging a reflective process, questioning of our body, and noticing what is present can lead to an experience of opening and transformation, understanding and appreciation furthered. The actions we take are not reactive but responsive.

Julie came to me after a partial mastectomy determined for the cancer to not return. She saw her diagnosis as a wake-up call to change her life and had already begun practicing yoga. As we worked together she questioned the cause of her cancer. She recognized breasts as what nurtured her two young children. When I asked how she nurtures herself, she brought up her hospitalization and chemotherapy treatment, then shifted the topic to her mom's refusal to take care of the children during her hospitalization and convalescence. When I pressed her further, she reluctantly admitted anger at her mom. The more she reflected, the more she recognized her mom's lack of compassion.

Her mom's disinterest in her grandchildren was nothing new. Over the years, she never acknowledged their birthdays nor asked about them on the phone. Julie acknowledged an uncomfortable truth about her mom, who had withheld affection and support throughout Julie's life. Julie associated moms as caring and loving and wanted to believe this true of hers, but it was far from the case. As she became honest with herself and reflected on the sting of her mom's repeated rejections, she recalled one event after another during her early years when her mom refused to make meals, forced her to wear shoes that no longer fit, and called her ugly and worse. The nurturing she continually wanted from her mom was never forthcoming. In recognizing the truth of her mom, Julie recognized the futility of her requests and consequently shifted the ways she nurtured herself.

A diagnosis of cancer or any other debilitating or life-threatening illness is far from a welcome experience. It may be among the greatest challenges of our life. It's what we do with the experience that matters. There is no one-size-fits-all response. Each body is unique. The challenge comes in getting to know our personal body, understanding its particular communication, navigating the turbulent waters of emotions, and shifting a perspective or modifying a behavior. The shift sets into motion a new pattern that supports the truth of who we are and who we can become.

Among the reasons for my involvement in healing has been to ease suffering. Years earlier, I foresaw a time when climate change and social instability increased distress and I wanted to be among those who provide relief, contribute to solutions, and inspire transformation. Too many suffer from anxiety, PTSD, and a weakened immune system. Too many are victims of domestic violence and an unhelpful health care system. Too many are traumatized by the destruction of their homes due to extreme weather and social volatility. Too many are controlled by the dictates of fear. A diverse biotic life essential to a habitable planet is at risk, its health and very existence intimately linked to our own. In my darkest moments it seems too late to right the sinking ship.

That's when panic sets in, even though I know the response helps no one. In those darkest of frightful moments, I inventory what's nearby: a sofa, a stack of books, windows, a home, food in the refrigerator, a loving spouse. This practice is for grounding, breaking free from the clutch of fear, and keeping the story of existence open-ended because none of us knows the moment or circumstance of our last breath. Being present is all there is. This moment. This breath. The practice readily bears fruit. A sigh rises up from my torso followed by a conclusion that all is well enough in the immediate environment and I've the focus and motivation for helpful actions. The warmth of love and compassion return. Taking appropriate action follows.

If wanted, I could have stuck with a path of fear—I need not go far to find a problem within and outside my home. Instead, my choice is to find a way to provide service and joy through healing, writing, dancing, gathering with heart-connected friends, strangers, and family, gratitude everywhere, a sowing of awe. In greater connection is possibility and hope. In greater connection are the fruits of our gifts and of love.

That said, this perilous moment in our history is a sign that our collective health and well-being have faltered miserably, the collective body communicating its imbalance. Similar to how personal pain and setbacks can be seen as an opportunity for change and growth, this collective moment, too, is offering itself up, none of it easy. Says economist Charles Eisenstein, "The present convergence of crises—in money, energy, education, health, water, soil, climate, politics, the environment, and more—is a birth crisis, expelling us from the old world into a new."[15] How we heed its call may be the difference between reducing or exacerbating suffering and contributing to a habitable or uninhabitable future. We can ignore and bandage what's most egregious or use our ailments for waking up, healing, and growing, essentially revamping entire systems. The dramatic challenges before us call for foundational change. These challenges are opportunities.

The way to any group is through an individual. Fortunately we all have access to one significant person, their name already in our contacts list with up-to-date phone number and address. That one person, the one with whom change is most likely to occur, the one with whom we exert the most influence, is ourselves. A way to improve upon oneself, to heal and initiate a transformation, is by identifying a neglected, bruised, and disowned part of us and pursuing steps for its integration. Identifying and getting to know that neglected part of us and treating ourselves with compassion strengthens our personal wholeness, our integrative intelligence, and the collective wholeness, those strengths accompanying us at home and work. To do anything less than respond to the call is a denial of life, a moral negligence. To transform a group, first we transform ourselves. We owe it to ourselves. We deserve to activate the full potential of our genes, to cultivate support, and contribute to conditions that enable thriving.

EMBRACING THE PRESENT

Heeding the call is the way forward and a friending of the present moment. Heeding the call summons the light and uplifts us toward opening our mind-body-energy-spirit for health and integrated presence. Doing so assists in dissolving ignorance and greed, fostering compassion, cultivating energetic awareness, respecting our planetary home, and transforming our quagmire of unease, disease, and isolation into conscious, radiant interconnections full of the exhilaration of aliveness.

It's a call to experience life with greater balance and to wake up from the slumber of limiting filters. It's a call for reflecting on the legacy of a heart. It's a reminder to treat all with care because the health of one person impacts another, and, well, it's a family thing, and we were all raised and graze in the same cosmos.

Satisfaction and bliss accompany our connecting with the inner fire of our being. We feel in alignment with our day-to-day activity, our energy in coherence with the heart and thought and being. We lose our health and wholeness if we perpetuate a state of depletion, if we fail to touch into what matters most. The body has a remarkable ability to heal itself and experience wholeness. What is the announcement or story your body is telling you in this moment? Its answers are contained in listening to your bones and your breath, the wind and stars, and your vitalizing energy. What happens when you tend to both the obvious and subtle phenomena of your body?

What keeps you going and what prevents you from engaging in the practices that best support you? How do you hold yourself back?

Try This

Make a list of activities that give you energy. As you write each item, notice how it makes you feel. Express gratitude toward yourself for each one. Make another list of activities that deplete your energy and notice how recording them makes you feel. With each item on this second list, include a statement that begins "I could . . ." There may be several for each item. Consider this a revision statement, where you change your perspective to a new possibility, a reframing with a potential solution that shifts your energy. For instance, perhaps you wrote food shopping as something that tires you. Here are some revision statements: I could go shopping with a friend. I could listen to my favorite music using my earbuds while shopping. I could find a store that delivers food to my door. What's interesting with the "I could's" is how alternatives appear, which subsequently shifts the energy.

Embracing health is a choice. Shifting our patterns away from dysfunction and limitation and taking a step toward improving our well-being restores our motivation, and we feel a bloom of renewal. If clueless about what that step might be, then the first step is to find out. It may be taking a nap or a trip, sitting quietly, or chatting with a friend.

Our body awaits our attention. It regularly elbows us to notice. It asks us to heal the split we perpetuate by alienating ourselves from the felt, grounded experience of ourselves. The dream of our body wants us to wake up. Our imagination is providing clues. There's no better time than now to look.

3

The Intelligence of Intuitive and Somatic Awareness

It is amazing how many hints and guides and intuitions
for living come to the sensitive person who has ears to hear
what his body is saying.

ROLLO MAY

While my Healing Touch teacher showed us hand placements to activate and balance biofield energy and stood near the massage table to watch our technique, she urged us to follow intuition. "If you receive a nudge or inspiration to alter the technique, do so," she said. "Follow your intuition. Learn the ways intuition manifests. Listen to the energy."

I might have welcomed the invitation wholeheartedly and embraced permission to bend the guidelines and follow my knowing. Instead I hesitated. Self-doubt stuck out its foot and I stumbled headfirst, body suspect. Years of writing and dancing had me continually bucking authority to connect with and establish my own voice. I reminded myself that the body and creative flow do not lie, their shifting landscape inviting us into their unfolding. My tendency included learning from the artistry of others, cultivating a signature style, and following personal impulses, the essence of creativity. Why the hesitation?

In pondering the cause of my doubt, I found a ready culprit in my eighth-grade algebra teacher, Mr. S., also the football coach. One Monday early in the school year he wrote the week's assignments on the blackboard, then swung around without setting down the chalk to tell us that the teacher next door would check on us while he was away. Yes, away. Not just for that day or that week but for the next several months. He would be leaving class to join players in the locker room and on the football field. As promised, the next-door teacher poked her head into the room each class meeting. We were a studious bunch who hunched over our desks, erasers and pencils in steady use. There was no need to scold us for getting out of our seat or tossing balled-up paper around the room for an improvised game of volleyball. Our sporadic chatter erupted only to confirm a page number or deliver a borrowed pencil sharpener, nothing more mischievous.

Numbers and their symbols contained an eloquent precision that intrigued me. There's no fudging a four if it's a five. Like the body when we take the time to connect with it, numbers do not lie. Numbers can be moved around but only fit together in limited places. I worked my way through the fun of each assignment. My method involved gazing at the problem until the answer appeared in my mind a few seconds later, showing up like the sun emerging from behind a cloud. I'd record the answer and check if it matched the one in the back of the book. It did. Every time. Then I worked out the process for reaching the answer, a method less laborious and clunky than the one described in the book. Not recognizing my method as unusual, I thought this was my algebraic mind at work. If I finished early, I moved on to history or English homework.

My method earned me a C on the test. It was the first time in my schooling that I earned a low grade, and it stung.

One class before he scurried out the door, I shuffled up to Mr. S.'s desk to question the grade, eager to learn what I was missing. Perhaps something with a variable.

"Your approach is not what's in the book," he said without a glance at my paper.

"But the answers are correct," I replied. "All of them."

"It's not what's in the book!" he said louder as if increased volume proved rightness. According to him, there was only one way to solve a problem, the book's way, and my way was wrong, despite it always leading to the correct answer.

Respectfully I asked, "Can you show me?"

"It's not important," he replied. Then the clincher: "Girls don't need to know math." He waved me dismissively back to my seat and into a gendered ghetto.

Boom. Door closed. The algebra door. And more.

THE IMBALANCE OF SEXISM

Imagine this: Men are told to smile regularly and keep their voices low to put everyone nearby at ease. No sullen, loud, or overly serious men welcome. They are pressured to take up small spaces, legs together, and to give the larger spaces to women for doing their thing, be it joking about the length of their hair or explaining how electricity works. Women require sizable areas to manage the weight of their power, voice, and know-how. They excel at calculating problems and solving difficulties, among the reasons they should be at the helm of the car, work, finances, family, and governance because men are—hmm, how shall I say this?—too emotional. Men are prone to jealousy, fits of anger, and hysteria. With highly sensitive egos, men put themselves first with little concern for the community. They are incapable of handling complex ideas.

I hope the previous paragraph with its absurdities disturbs you and raises your hackles. Yet many of the particulars are common stereotypes applied in reverse. Girls and women have been told versions of this message repeatedly. To please and appease is everything, we're told. Except that it's not, unless this please and appease includes respect, empowerment, and wisdom as sturdy as a well-built house with a garden and well-maintained roadways and bridges nearby.

Implied in the notion of please and appease is a pattern of seeking approval and operating from subservience. Patriarchy historically regards men as the stronger of the sexes who therefore should dominate in all areas from the bedroom to the boardroom. This paradigm, or filter, operates as all filters do, by omitting key information and perspectives. Among alternatives to patriarchal dominance, how about connection and growth, collaboration and synergy? How about mutual respect?

Over the years, I've shared my math story with colleagues. They wonder why I did not press Mr. S. further for an explanation or complain to a principal or my parents about his overt sexism. This was the seventies, and few of my teachers embraced the social changes launched in the sixties with its burgeoning equalities for women. Only the year before, my adviser prevented me from pursuing my interest in cars and engines through taking shop class by steering me instead into home economics for its practical skills of baking muffins and knitting.

In home economics, I was instructed to wear a bright-yellow apron tied at the waist and measure flour by the cupful for the purpose of the perfectly sized, tasty muffin. There was nothing about resource allocation, economizing resources, or learning how the chemistry of baking soda reacts with acids in the dough, which results in carbon dioxide, any of which would have interested me far more. A muffin was neither a current or projected part of my diet and much less practical than learning about an engine, essential to my highly anticipated driver's license and imminent slide into the driver's seat of my parents' car. As instructed for knitting, I chose two colors of yarn skeins for a vest to coordinate with one of my skirts, though I did not see the point of knitting for hours when it was easier to buy a finished product at a department store. Nor was this Mindfulness 101 with the teacher emphasizing awareness of breath, thoughts, and emotions in a reciprocal dance with the needles and yarn. My curiosity latched on to what propelled a car into motion, not making a tight or loose stitch or finding the right blend of flour and granulated sugar. As a result, my attention regularly wandered outside the classroom to a passing car or wasp hitting the window, which prompted my muffins to burn and my vest to come out with mismatched arm holes. I ate a few bites of my muffins and unraveled my vest back to its initial, untantalizing fiber and went no further with each. My neglected, substandard projects earned me a surprising A.

If I had more confidence and my current teacher know-how, I might have scraped my chair along the floor until reaching Mr. S.'s desk and implored him to demonstrate the value of the book's method over mine. Instead believing my algebra skills hopeless, I avoided taking another math class during high school, relieved when the mandate for trigonometry and calculus arrived after my graduation.

Years later while flipping through television channels, I happened upon the last minutes of a PBS program on algebra and listened to the voiceover with animated equations demonstrate not the rudimentary steps of the book but my method, which was described as advanced. I lingered on the show, unwilling to move from the couch until the roll of credits, the show laying bare Mr. S.'s misinformation and misguided discouragement. The damage was already done, however, and my only boastworthy math ability today is my avoidance of tasks that include numbers beyond the basics of addition and subtraction performed thankfully with the assistance of a calculator.

I could go on and on about the What Ifs. I'll indulge in a few. What if Mr. S. pulled out the chair beside his desk for us to talk? What if he showed interest in my method and we shared an involved math conversation? What if he suggested another book to read? What if he steered me into calculus? What if he encouraged me to trust my voice, natural ability, and vision? What if he valued the intelligence of girls as much as he did the physical prowess of boys?

Many women have told me various versions of my story, the classroom in another part of the country, the teacher bearded, the admonition accompanied by a note home about the student's misconduct. I'm delighted by the exceptions, the women whose stories include encouragement to pursue math and embrace fields like physics, chemistry, and engineering, their interest and talents recognized.

Like many women, the #MeToo movement has stirred my anger at numerous instances of recalling an inappropriate grab, lewd comment, or work getting ignored. Most women have a lengthy list of grievous stories of being overlooked, belittled, held back, and abused, our opinions and contributions mattering less than those of our male counterparts. We get noticed, but often for the wrong reasons. It seems we come in handy for a man's projection of frustration, anger, and other unexamined, disowned emotions that boil into a toxic stew, their emotional intelligence abysmally poor. Male rage upon spouses or romantic partners is unfortunately commonplace. A 2018 report reveals that 35 percent of women worldwide end up the recipient of a man's aggression, with about 38 percent of murders of women committed by a male partner.[1] These figures are so large, having increased during the COVID pandemic, that the World Health Organization considers violence against women a major public health problem. With the 2020 world population at approximately 8.7 billion, that means about 3,045,000,000 women are victims of violence, a figure that competes with the burning of witches in Europe in the fifteenth and sixteenth centuries when many a village killed anywhere from half to the entire population of its women.

WHEN A SMILE ISN'T ENOUGH

Although no blood was spilled, I want to unpack my algebra story not for its wound to my self-esteem, but for its societal ramifications. There is a price to be paid for steering women toward muffins and vests and silencing us in other areas.

First is its blatant sexism. Not alone in his perspective, Mr. S. followed the popular cultural bias that promoted mathematical thinking as a domain reserved for boys and men. Girls were excluded from this club for the singular crime of not carrying a Y chromosome. Gender stereotypes reinforced boys excelling in employing this numeric language, being better equipped at manipulating abstract and spatial ideas and handling tools. Girls were thought to excel at soft sciences such as psychology and sociology and to be better at relationships, a well-baked and -served muffin apparently a bonding essential. Boys urged to pursue math received accolades for doing so as did girls who went into caretaking professions like nursing. A pattern present in several of my classes was implied bias, which is a behavior applied unconsciously based on stereotypes that can lead, for instance, to teachers favoring a boy with his hand up over a girl, a selection that when repeated often enough reinforces a boy's ability and confidence while discouraging a girl's. I learned that raising my hand was an exercise in futility, like a flag of an outlying, resourceless country, the desk or my lap eventually receiving my resentful hands. Over the years, I've seen a similar pattern in meetings in which the men spoke out freely, sometimes with misplaced confidence, explaining and interrupting, while the women politely waited for a pause or invitation to speak that sometimes never happened.

Exclusion from the math club has been a common phenomenon among women worldwide. Fortunately, in a period of change, the old-school way of thinking clashing with the new as is apparent in comments by career economist and Harvard President Lawrence Summers. In 2005 he asserted gendered difference resulting from genetics, not conditioning, privilege, or socioeconomic factors as the reason few women excelled in math and science. He received quite a backlash when he talked about women's lack of interest in analytical fields and reluctance to work long hours because of maternal interests and day care needs.[2] That he was asked to resign as a result of his comments is a telling indication of shifting attitudes.

With any stereotype, there is some truth to its generalization. Many studies in neuroscience, for instance, show that the male brain is more active in the left hemisphere, the area devoted to logic, precision, and facts. The female brain has more right hemisphere activity, the area of receptivity, creativity, imagination, and feelings. Tellingly, the right side is also involved in intuition, but I'll get to that shortly. Women also tend to utilize their corpus callosum, the region responsible for both hemispheres being in dialogue, more frequently than men. Developmental psychologist Carol Gilligan sees differences in how women and men think—that women rely on relationships and belonging while men prize autonomy and hierarchy. Interestingly, she also sees that all develop similarly through four stages: care of self; care toward a specific group; care toward all people; and integrated, where men and women think alike.[3] Ultimately, the good news is that the emotional and interpersonal intelligences for both men and women are equally conducive to developing, revealing our brain as malleable and our abilities as adaptive.

To a degree, a stereotype is helpful by enabling us to understand complex information quickly. It's the sound bite of the nightly news, the quickly composed tweet, or the Cliffs Notes that come in handy when we're pressed for time and attention and we need an easily digestible summary. But it's the same reason that renders it problematic and misleading. The simplification leaves out vital details. The omissions lead to a misrepresentation of information and erroneous conclusions. It leads to believing men behave one way, women quite another, a Venus and Mars dichotomy in which never the two craniums shall meet and share any gray and white matter with its billions of nerves that make speaking, listening, reading, and other activities possible. It leads to hunkering down in unhelpful divisiveness and reinforcing an outdated status quo.

Stereotypes are inherently flawed through their partial truth and simplistic perspectives. They harm by leading to assumptions that an individual can fit comfortably into a prefabricated idea. They harm by okaying what gets overlooked and promoting a willful blindness to the beliefs and ideals that don't fit the simple mold.

Gender stereotypes assume an indisputable distinction between a man and a woman. Most societies, with exceptions such as the Bugis of Sulawesi, Indonesia, view sex as binary with two rigidly fixed options, male or female, based on a person's reproductive functions, genitals, sex chromosomes, gonads, and hormones. This common sex binary fails to recognize a third category, intersex, individuals with a combination of male and female biological characteristics. The American Psychological Association believes that as many as 1 in 1,500 babies are born with ambiguous genitalia.[4] With the U.S. population at 330,000,000, this means approximately 220,000 people, the equivalent of the number of people living in a city the size of Spokane, Washington. The number of intersex individuals suggests that differences more realistically fall along a biological spectrum, a reason that there are new categories such as gender fluid and nonbinary that have made their way into the mainstream. Additionally, gender binaries do not consider the impact of culture, upbringing, and socioeconomic background. Nor do they consider the influence of embodied practices upon consciousness. In short, there are exceptions. Many of them. No one fits exactly into conventional definitions of masculine or feminine. Trying to squeeze our myriad qualities into one or the other is harmful individually and collectively.

Implied biases, any unconsciously held associations about a group, influence how we come to knowing and how we determine what is acceptably knowable. Such biases erode confidence, limit options, and stifle innovation. Bias closes doors. It teaches girls and women to stay out of the boys' club and, as was the case in Victorian times, retreat to the parlor to refrain from worldly conversation to focus instead on idle domestic talk. It's not that long ago that Western women were encouraged to hide unladylike behavior such as reading, writing, and pursuing advanced education. Critics of Mary Shelley's 1818 work, *Frankenstein,* refused to believe that such a bold novel that married science and imagination could have been written by a woman. The conservative London publication *A British Critic* attacked Shelley by saying, "The writer of it is, we understand, a female; this is an aggravation of that which is the prevailing fault of the novel; but if our authoress can forget the gentleness of her sex, it is no reason why we should; and we shall therefore dismiss the novel without further comment."[5] Up until 1974, not that long ago, women were routinely denied credit cards without a husband or father as a cosigner.

We can laugh at the antiquated sentiments and prohibitions, but there's still many a glass ceiling yet to be broken. Though greatly improved, writing is still not a field that embraces women. Publishing continues to be a domain favoring men as shown by VIDA, the feminist organization that reports on gender disparities in major literary publications and book reviews. For instance, their 2019 assessment of *The New York Review of Books* revealed women as 33.37 percent of their contributors, slightly up from previous years.[6] Scholar and classicist Mary Beard in *Women and Power: a Manifesto* writes at length about the legion of male trolls that viciously pounce upon a woman writer when her work reaches into the mainstream and plucks a nerve. Great imbalances in opportunities are apparent worldwide, with women needing to seek permission to travel abroad (Saudi Arabia), pursuing an education beyond middle school (Afghanistan), or making important decisions without consulting a father or brother (South Korea and numerous other countries). The United States has yet to open the White House doors to a female president, which I hope will no longer be the case within my lifetime.

Equally telling is the percentage of men outnumbering women in leadership positions. Of the CEOs who led companies on the 2018 Fortune 500 list, only twenty-four, or 4.8 percent, are women.[7] Leadership experts Robert J. Anderson and William A. Adams say it's far too few. Studies they've reviewed led them to conclude that women lead more effectively and creatively than men and get better results from all involved, contradicting what many may be quick to believe.[8]

There's something seriously wrong with a picture of humanity that slights half the world population. Limiting educational opportunities to one segment of the human population means lost opportunities, not just for women but for all. The World Bank, who counters lost opportunities financially, determined in a 2018 report that excluding girls from education costs between fifteen trillion and thirty trillion dollars, figures that take into account earnings and standards of living, child marriage and early childbearing, fertility and population growth, health, nutrition and well-being, agency and decision-making, and social capital and institutions.[9] Other studies show that poverty significantly decreases when women receive microloans. Interestingly women invest funding in family and community, whereas men apparently devote a portion of those funds toward alcohol consumption.[10]

What makes sexism particularly heinous, the part that is so difficult to wrap my mind around, is its central tenet of misogyny—the disdain, prejudice, and hatred toward women. For the record, I would say the same if a similar contempt were directed against men. But here's a significant, perhaps overlooked point: Misogyny's venom is not only directed at women but extends as well to men who commit the crime of exhibiting characteristics and behaviors considered feminine. Men are discouraged from exhibiting feminine qualities and conditioned against feeling emotions that reveal vulnerability. No crying allowed, as one too many boys have been told, a prohibition that wreaks havoc on their emotional intelligence and boxes them into the one of few emotions welcomed: anger.

Essentially, qualities considered feminine are under assault regardless of who exhibits them. Women are denigrated for being womanly and men are shamed for exhibiting any qualities deemed feminine. Among the insults hurled at men are being called a "sissy," "pussy," or "throwing like a girl," all of which challenge their manhood and point to their inability to "man up." Sexist stereotypes on full display, some people have told me that I think like a man, considered a compliment or insult depending on the messenger, and that I walk like a man (this from a Malaysian taxi driver commenting on my interest in and ability to hike for miles).

Masculine strength becomes dysfunctional, a weakness, or a hazard when it becomes the default response that excludes other responses. Men are robbed of a rich emotional life if limiting ideas of masculinity are imposed. Women are similarly robbed of abilities from narrow ideas of femininity that leave out options like being forthright or commanding. All are robbed of accessing the fullness of who we are.

Misogyny worsens matters by its excessive celebration of masculine qualities to the exclusion of, denigration of, and violence toward feminine qualities. The ideology justifies the oppression of females while inflating the value of masculinity, healthy for no one. With a disregard for balance essential to personal and collective well-being and a denial that we each harbor some combination of male and female traits, it justifies a paradigm of domination. It establishes a pattern of one group or idea at the helm subordinating another group, groups, or ideas. It supports epistemicide, wherein the dominant group, out of a need to control a narrative, omits other perspectives, does not reveal insecurities, and will minimize—even annihilate—an entire system of knowledge. It's what propagates internalized oppression and self-harm. It encourages separating ourselves from shameful qualities and shutting down parts of us, which leads to dissociation from the body and what surrounds us. It's what births imperialism and tyranny and closes down dialogue. Its celebration births crop homogenization, which destroys microbial diversity in soil. It's what contributes to land subjected to domination, the decimation of an oxygen producing forest, an overabundance of greenhouse gases, and the forced removal of indigenous people. It's what ignores or erodes naturalist and ecological intelligences. It pushes intuition and other potential beneficial perspectives into a ghetto. It's what leads to imbalance and irrationality and lowers the quality of life not just for the subjugated group, but for all.

A DYSFUNCTIONAL TILT

A domination paradigm may look good on paper, especially for the group in power who receives immediate benefits, but restrictions can hold up for only so long. Eventually emotional, socioeconomic, and ecological levees break and destructive repercussions previously held back or kept hidden bust out and nature reclaims balance. That eventuality, with protests about sexism, racism, economic inequities, and environmental policies, is occurring now.

The dysfunctional masculine raising its belligerent head in a patriarchal order overvalues individualism, how well we differentiate ourselves and act from independence and self-reliance. We believe these qualities indicate strength, which they do but only to a degree. If done without reflection and understanding ramifications, without a recognition of the value of balance, be it masculine qualities with feminine, speaking but also listening, acting but also reflecting, it contributes to hyperindividualism. It leads to a bellicose egotism so inflated and self-focused that it ignores the value of connection, empathy, collaboration, and interconnectivity. The imbalance contributes to isolation, alienation, anxiety, and depression, and cuts us off from the totality of who we are. We become lopsided, entrenched in a limiting perspective, a rigidity with detrimental effects on individual and collective bodies.

We can all benefit from reflection and an honest appraisal of self, which is what prompted the following list of personality qualities. As you read them, notice your reaction. Which qualities feel positive and which negative? Which provoke admiration or contempt?

A	B
strong	gentle
independent	deferential
decisive	patient
courageous	nurturing
assertive	receptive
firm	sensitive
brazen	quiet
unemotional	emotional
analytical	intuitive

If not obvious, the lists categorize stereotypical behavior most commonly associated with the male (A) and female (B) binary. Sexist attitudes relish the qualities in A for a man and consider those in B as inferior or best if they appear in women. I would hope few of us subscribe to such stereotypes and welcome these qualities regardless of who they show up in and value them based on circumstance. All things in balance. Some situations require brazenness and others require quiet. Decisiveness is helpful unless we rush headstrong into a decision without considering impact. It's good to speak up but essential also to listen. Sensitivity is a strength unless firmness is more appropriate. It's a matter of recognizing which quality best serves a situation. Discerning a situation, combining heart with mind, is a sign of wisdom and developed emotional and somatic intelligence.

This discussion is intended to move us closer to a more comprehensive and mature appreciation of masculinity and femininity and toward an expanded and integrative bodymind. This is a reminder to trust sensations, thoughts, and feelings, to use the brain and the heart, to explore all of who we are and can be, and to develop our interests and inclinations wisely, all the more important as we aim to address colossal challenges smartly. This is an invitation to consider and be in dialogue with multiple perspectives. This is a call to step out of personal and societal limits and remove the filters that no longer serve the greater good. This is a call to grow into our potential, to be more *telerotic,* a combination of "telos" and "eros," a word coined by futurist Barbara Marx Hubbard, which she says means "to fall in love with the fulfillment of the potential of the whole. I've . . . always been attracted to emergent possibilities, the telos inherent in evolution towards higher consciousness and greater complexity. So telerotic for me means to fall in love with the universe becoming more complex, more aware, and more self-aware."[11] Ultimately this is a call to tend to the soil of our being.

We are all composites of feminine and masculine qualities. To reject any one of the qualities on the list above due to sexism—or any other provincial, discriminatory idea—is to malign ourselves. This maligning, or internalized oppression, may manifest as not resting when tired, pushing through stress rather than addressing the cause, and dismissing intuition, new thought, or any other emergent, potentially helpful idea. Rejecting any parts poisons our being, energy, and spirit and cuts off access to the full range of our abilities. Such restrictions stifle our ability to act from a healthy, compassionate, creative, fluid, synergetic, and integrated center. The flow of our vitalizing energy slows down or stops altogether.

To be our most complete, mature, empowered, and realized self means accepting all of who we are. This means listening to what prompts shame and pride, joy and sadness, hurt and courage. Each has its gifts, some more readily apparent than the others. Acceptance also means there's room to improve. It's not a free pass to act injudiciously without reflection. Far from it. Acceptance is an essential step in embodiment. It roots us in the felt experience of our being, away from abstracting and conceptualizing, and toward emotional, energetic, somatic, and spiritual intelligences. It expands the field of consciousness. Acknowledging What Is and facing reality however wondrous, frightening, convoluted, and awesome it may appear is the fertile ground for growth.

Consider what happens in reframing masculine and feminine as yin and yang, inhale and exhale, summer and winter, or high and low tide. What comes to the foreground is recognizing the necessity of each as an essential partnership and cyclical necessity. One is dependent on the other, a pattern of rhythmic reciprocity visible in nature. A bee needs the nectar as much as the flower needs the bee. Many a seed needs a cold season for germination. Sometimes a situation requires us to be assertive; other times it needs us to step back and listen. Like our sympathetic and parasympathetic nervous systems, vitality and strength depend on a flow between opposing forces coming together, separating, and coming together, responsive to circumstances.

THE INTELLIGENCE OF INTUITION

Which brings me to intuition, a powerful intelligence for sensing, knowing, and growing, and an area of concern that arose from my algebra slighting. What ways of knowing are utilized and validated and which are overlooked? Does one organ of our senses and type of perception get privileged over another? How are we limiting or harming ourselves if we overlook a type of perception?

Intuition is a sudden knowing that bypasses the usual processing of the senses. It may appear as a vision or be felt as a subtle bodily sensation. This sudden knowing pops into awareness like an impromptu waking dream, as a hunch, gut feeling shiver, or unbidden voice. It shows up out of nowhere, the source and trail of causality unclear. It seems to operate by rules that defy logic and ignore the usual space-time constructs connected to linear sequencing. It may deliver information from miles away through none of the common channels like a telephone, instead riding on an invisible, imperceptible circuitry until, that is, it arrives with a subtle or obvious nudge.

Intuition often speaks in a symbolic language akin to dream imagery and aligns with the deep, bodily knowing of instinct. It may be explicable by quantum entanglement in which particles appear and disappear with no recognizable causal connection or proximity, among the phenomena that Einstein referred to as "spooky action at a distance."[12] It may also be the working of the enteric brain and the thirty neurotransmitters continually sending messages from the gut to our head via the vagus nerve.

I attribute my approach to solving algebra equations to intuition. My method was neither premeditated nor calculated. It rose on its own, reliably delivering the solutions as a flash of knowing. It worked like a high-speed internet connection, whereas the textbook relied on a connection speed painfully slower than dial-up. It appeared like any innate ability like breathing or a seed breaking open to send its shoot upward through the dirt toward sunlight. The need to complete my homework and the lack of in-class instruction created ripe conditions to provoke it into action.

Intuition comes naturally to a child who has not yet been fully conditioned by culture and is free to focus on imagination and play. A child not yet roped into cultural shoulds pursues what engages her attention moment to moment and engages in flow. A child follows her curiosity and willingly goes where it takes her. Intuition appeared unquestioned in several areas during my early years, in the stories and poems penned into a journal kept in my bedroom drawer and in explorations of the acres of woods behind my family home when the call of a stream, the wind, sunlight, or a robin pulled me out of the house to wander the wilderness of the land and my mind, no fence keeping me out.

Intuition pooh-poohs restrictions. It goes where it wants to go and passes through walls of common limitations. It abides by its own rules apart from reason, logic, and familiarity. It shows up if we're patient and receptive, if we let it manifest in the form of its choosing, if we surrender a preference for holding on to preconceived outcomes. Later in this chapter, I'll share a story about distant healing that shattered my preconceptions, but let me continue with this discussion on intuition first.

Entertaining intuition requires trust. It functions best when we let go of the need to control and the belief that nothing is possible unless the ego or will makes it happen. Instead it asks us to twist the lens of our filters to a more open attention and align ourselves with the present moment. It asks us to practice neutral awareness and to tune in to the senses. It's a matter of defining an intent, then to wait, wonder, and witness, frequently operating on a timetable not of our choosing.

How intuition manifests is often based upon which of our senses dominates, whether our mode of learning is based on, for instance, sound, touch, or vision. My client Jill connects with her intuition by using her nondominant hand to write. She poses a question for which she wants an insight, writing it down with her right hand and then switches hands to write the reply. She has used it to make major decisions like whether or not to return to school and claims the technique always steers her well. Katy used intuition to locate a new house. Her realtor kept leading her to houses that fell short of the criteria that she and her husband wanted. One day, she got in the car and let a gut feeling lead her to a house that her realtor hadn't mentioned but helped her close on several weeks later.

Although my algebra teacher's neglect and comment set up a barrier that instilled doubt and prompted me to turn away from math, it fortunately did not shut down my intuition altogether. I've experienced enough intuitive and uncommon phenomenon over the years that I can solicit feedback when needed, as happened during a hike in

New York's Adirondack Mountains with my friend. After hours of a grueling walk on uneven stones in a stream bed, my energy was plummeting. My pace had slowed, the passing flowers no longer caught my attention, and I struggled to maintain a steady footing on the loose stones. When we emerged from the cool of the tree cover to a blaze of sun and a sizable cliff that would have to be scaled, my heart temporarily seized and the scant saliva in my mouth turned to sand. "I thought this was the easy trail," I complained, which prompted my friend to pull out the map and determine he had led us mistakenly onto a difficult trail. He offered the choice of doubling back on the eight arduous miles or scaling the cliff and walking another four miles of yet unseen terrain. Neither option held appeal. I needed water that we no longer had, a long rest preferably on a soft surface, and something to quell my trembles and lightheadedness. Lacking confidence in my ability to climb the cliff without placing us in danger, I imagined locking my fingers and feet into an available crevice and losing my grip and falling. But I also did not believe myself capable of retracing the eight miles that had already consumed the majority of the day. We had two hours of daylight left, and those hours shriveled to feel more like minutes.

Suddenly the ground pulled me down like a magnet, standing no longer an option. I began stroking the dirt and stone in an unfamiliar frenzy, kicking both into the air to land on my face and in my hair. Then all grew oddly quiet, peaceful, and dreamlike, and my motion stilled. In the welcome lull, I silently asked if I would survive the cliff. The answer came immediately, a voice replying resoundingly with a reassuring yes. A few hours later, I stumbled into camp in the dark like a zombie and slipped into our tent for a long, deep sleep.

It's valuable to recognize the difference between intuition, which is helpful information and guidance, from fantasy and wishful or delusional thinking. Intuition is not susceptible to the manipulation of our ego or emotion. Intuition persists despite our preference for a specific outcome. Its knowing cuts through biases and preferences. It can be direct like a tactless friend who unapologetically blurts out what's on his mind. It may be a fleeting quizzical sensation, a hunch, or a flash noticeable only if attentive—emphasis on *if.*

To become familiar with intuition, it helps to notice bodily reactions and anomalous impressions, to develop trust and withhold judgment, to meditate, to be alert to mood changes, to take calculated risks, to keep a journal of anticipated and actual outcomes, to find expression through creative expression. It helps to maintain a childlike curiosity. Like any skill, developing intuition requires practice.

When I engage with a client's energy for healing, intuition often guides my hand placements and provides images informing me about what is taking place with their body and biofield. It's an ingredient in the energy that courses through my spine and fascia connecting me to something beyond the boundary of my skin. It's the information hovering nearby awaiting my attention and compelling me to engage on a deep sensory level that surpasses the limits of reason and ready understanding. It's the pull that gets me turning left when my direction has been straight. It gets me to pause during a walk or chat with a friend because it arrives unexpectedly and summons my attention, a reason a small notebook accompanies me regularly. Intuition is the images and inspiration that feed my writing and dance and enable one phrase to follow another. Medical researcher Jonas Salk, who developed one of the earliest polio vaccines, has said that "reason is what we use to convince ourselves of what our intuition has already told us."[13]

Intuition first, thinking after.

Intuition gets us to bend toward the sun or away. To sit beneath the maple tree, not alongside the stream. To hear not only the fury of our mind, but its whispers. To notice the shadow of the moon and the world to come.

Notably, intuition, an abundant, valuable resource of wisdom, insight, and healing, is sometimes referred to as women's intuition or a women's way of knowing because women tend to access it more readily than men. Such framing might be considered complimentary in its appreciation of a quality common to women. But in a sexist culture that devalues women, the term carries a derogatory connotation. Intuition gets demeaned as suspect, questionable, untrustworthy, and illogical, and those who follow it are considered ridiculous, witchy, or worse. Intuition does not receive a five-star rating as compared to logic and reason, which reinforces masculine ways of knowing.

No surprise that the main subjects in school emphasize logic, which is based on the inclination of the male brain. Logic, deductive and reductive analysis, and reasoning are considered foundational to a solid education. Such approaches to knowing support the scientific method—these are the scaffolding for math and the framework for grammar. Excelling in these areas sends you to the head of the class and opens doors to a respected and financially rewarding career.

In contrast, subjects that utilize intuition such as art, dance, music, writing, and drama—essentially classes where creativity plays a significant role—are considered superfluous and expendable. Those excelling in these areas may be nice enough people, a backhanded compliment that implies a degree of foolishness or elitism and is ultimately insulting. The doors that open for those pursuing these fields come with substantially less respect and financial reward.

We neglect intuition and privilege logic to our detriment. It places us at risk of being short-sighted, ignorant, and half-brained (literally), and missing out on vital information. It's akin to favoring the left leg over the right leg or one arm over the other. Sure, one arm may be better at grasping, but the other arm may excel at stabilizing. Abilities like lifting a heavy box and playing the piano are best performed with both hands. It's foolhardy to favor one part of the brain and leave an entire region of gray matter underutilized. Sending satellites into space and probing the inner space of the mind and body both generate useful discoveries. Why not explore the science of intuition, the art of logic, and the many dimensions of knowing?

Favoring one type of cognition disregards a more complete knowing and its resulting outcomes. Relying on only a single segment of the brain and perceptions misses out on a larger picture of what is knowable. Operating from bias limits thought and feeling, potential cut by our half-brained, gender-biased cultural notions. We lose out if intuition is shamed into exile. Similarly we lose out if we rely upon it exclusively. Purposefully ignoring an ability is foolhardy, especially now with current existential challenges. Logic and intuition are great bedfellows and valid ways of knowing. It's not an either/or but both. Logic and intuition work hand in hand, one going where the other cannot. Together they generate a powerful alliance, a stronger intelligence than is possible when relying only on one. Both serve valuable functions.

Try This

Walk slowly around your room or a nearby space. Intend to let your eyes be drawn to something. It could be the wall, the shape of the lamp, or how the shade shares and conceals light. Linger in place longer than you might otherwise. Watch what shifts, what new details emerge. Follow your attention and what captures it the most. How does that detail inform you about another area of your life?

This exercise loosens attention to see what more wants to come through. Watch with your gut. Use your inner eyes. Invite breath into places your awareness rarely goes. Feel the support of the earth through your feet.

Combining logic with intuition contributes to connective, systemic, comprehensive, and integrative awareness. Pathways open up. Perceptions expand. Innovative solutions and insights arrive. Combine intuition and logic regularly and patterns of connections on micro and macro levels become visible. We come to see that a singular act is not an isolated event but contains immediate and distant ramifications. Similarly it's not just me to you or you to me, but a mutual relationship of us with them and them with them, a vast interconnected, interdependent web of atoms, cells, ganglion, and bacteria, one ideology alongside another, one biofield wave alongside another, a unified field, every one of our actions and thoughts rippling into another, from person to planet and back.

When an intuitive hit arrives, I greet it with awe but also a snippet of suspicion to determine if it is helpful or harmful. I consult my gut with its potent neurotransmitters, the enteric nervous system more capable of detecting danger and deceit better than any other organ. Practice reinforces coming to recognize and trust the myriad ways intuition shows up and the importance of intention and openness. Ask, wait, and witness. Be open to experiencing intuition upon whatever sensory channel it arrives.

Knowing intuition implies a done deal, but such a conclusion can close us off to processing new information accurately. Too much or too little confidence toward this stream of knowing pollutes its information. Both leave us susceptible to mistakes, presumption, conceptualization, and analysis, which distance us from sensory presence and a disregard for the evidence before us. Intuition arrives via the senses but also takes dramatic leaps, the brain processing phenomena faster than the mind. It's pivotal to find the middle ground between trust and doubt, between receptivity and analysis, to land upon truth.

Intuition led me to use imagination on Hal, the client I wrote about in the previous chapter who had come to me with depression and chronic pressure on his chest that no doctor was able to relieve. An intuitive hunch urged me to work with him using imagination, to cocreate with him the imagined bathtub scene and access a broader range of conscious and unconscious material. Imagination allowed me to build upon the material he presented without holding to it literally.

Engaging imagination's malleable, dreamlike state loosened emotional and mental energy, which upended a habitual pattern manifesting as chest pain. Prior to working with Hal, I hadn't incorporated imagination as overtly into my healing approach, but the positive results with him prompted me to engage the tool of imagination with others who have similarly experienced positive outcomes. A moment's hunch pursued has led me to appreciating imagination effectiveness in healing, a way to engage energy and come to knowing.

INTEGRATIVE KNOWING

Common knowing privileges logic, reasoning, and head-centered knowing. Missing is a comprehensive sense of the body that includes intuition, embodiment, energetic, and spiritual awareness that is integrative rather than fractional. Missing is a place and appreciation for uncanny experiences and impressions that don't readily fit into our belief system. A comprehensive understanding of the body recognizes us as a combination of physical and electromagnetic matter, as particles, waves, atoms, cells, fluids, and flesh. Intuition draws from the entirety of the body. Similarly embodiment draws from the physical and the less densely mattered body. Integrative knowing supports us seamlessly shifting gears from one mode of perception to another. A nervous system's health increases when it is inclusive, blossoming with direct sensory experience and input from the biofield, synaptic pathways forming and reforming.

The body relishes this fluid engagement. Just this moment. Just this hunch or touch or smell or seeing. Just this pause as a flow of the conscious and the unconscious come to light. No intermediaries. Engage on this more primal level before turning to thinking and the analytical brain, before what is sensed gets translated conceptually, before the uncanny nuances of felt experiences get left on the editing room floor and a perceptible shift takes place.

Integrative knowing engages the cellular level and gets all systems humming far away from the cul-de-sac of an overreliance on intellectual knowing, which can, if we let it dominate, if we let it pretend to be the be-all and end-all, have us endlessly circling thought, each circumnavigation a further distancing from our body, self, being, community, and environment. What gets lost is sensory awareness and smooth complete breaths. Lost, too, is feeling rooted in the present moment so integral to what is now unfolding. A further loss is an open channel to intuition. Note that this is not a call for its dismissal. Head-centric knowing is highly useful but becomes problematic when other types of knowing are ignored, when one hand knows nothing of the actions or abilities of any other limb or organ.

It's easy to determine which of my clients are head centered and disconnected from their body. Often their hearts feel closed and their body appears stiff. It's as if their flesh mindlessly tags behind them like a car trailer careening with every turn, its wheels banging into curbs while the oblivious driver takes a consequent turn. These clients explain a circumstance by describing a symptom. My probe for further details reveals little. When I ask about felt experience, they look blankly and say they don't understand the question. I'm not asking them to understand, only to feel. Daniel came to me with high blood pressure and depression. The side effects of medications he took for them left him tired, which compounded his already low motivation for his graphic design work. He became slightly animated when he spoke about his enjoyment of jazz.

"Where do you feel the music in your body," I asked, to which he responded with a blank look. "How does it feel when I place my hands on your shoulders and have you lift your arms?" Another blank look. "What's the temperature of my hands?"

"I know I should feel something, but there's nothing," he replied, his voice a lackluster drone. No delight or shame, no heat, cool, or shortness of breath, only a bewildering nothing.

I might have well asked how it was to go running with a snail. He would have given me the same despondent look. I could feel fear and emotion locked away in a hinterland of his body. A locked-down response is common among trauma survivors who detach from feeling and block hurtful memories of the event. At the time of the offense, the body copes by constricting and withdrawing, as if tucking its tail between its legs and shuffling off to a corner, sometimes bolting the door shut. Yet feelings not dealt with persist by taking up lasting residence in the flesh and can contribute to, among other complications, an overproduction of cortisol, which deleteriously impacts health, the reason so many trauma survivors end up with an autoimmune disease. The blocked feelings can influence us in other ways, too, unconsciously sabotaging relationships and work. Some of us may never move out from the corner and access the valuable but locked off parts of ourselves. Daniel admitted to no trauma history—or chose not to disclose it with me. He stopped coming after a few sessions, and when I ran into him twenty-five pounds thinner a year later, he told me he survived a recent heart attack and was battling prostate cancer.

In turning attention to the entirety of the body, rooting in sensation and entertaining the ways we perceive, an interesting shift takes place. We engage the process of embodiment. Embodiment is an ongoing process. It's not an activity done once like filing taxes, which most of us do once a year. Like eating or sleeping, which the body requires performed daily to function well, embodiment requires regular attention. It's a practice of awakening to who we are moment to moment, to listening deeply with mind and body, eyes and ears, imagination and senses. It's a process of settling into the residence of our body.

SOMATIC INTELLIGENCE

The flesh of our being is continually sending messages and revealing itself. It's up to us to attend to the myriad phenomenon and come to know the idiosyncrasies of our flesh and to increase our somatic literacy. We get curious. We notice. We're not looking at the body from a distance, as an object and abstraction. We're not static like a chair. Instead attention focuses on sensing what is taking place in the moment. We may sweat, experience an itch, tremble, or feel weary, joy, or longing. We may detect tightness in the chest, coolness at the back of the neck, fleeting sadness. An image may appear that may be a memory or be symbolic of what is taking place. Your eyes following these words may move quickly or slow down at a specific passage as you change your position and lean back from this line. A phenomenon not registered previously may show up. It may have been there all along, but you took until now to notice, off stage, unconscious material becoming conscious. When I lead my students in awareness exercises, they are stunned to hear the whoosh of the air conditioner or the jeer of the blue jay out the window, both present since the start of class, but taking until doing an exercise for them to hear. Even a few minutes of deliberate sensing initiates a shift toward embodiment, which they greet as a welcome surprise.

The body as object leads to knowing that blood makes up about 8 percent of our body weight and that the brain, if necessary, can withstand being without oxygen for as long as ten minutes. The body as object leads to knowing that the heart beats approximately one hundred thousand times per day and our trillions of cells continually absorb nutrients from our cereal, sandwich, and whatever else makes its way onto the day's menu. These fascinating facts about the body uncovered by science could keep me entertained for hours, especially if the book or website comes with color illustrations. But a thousand articles or books about the body will not increase embodiment. There's only one way, through personal, firsthand, subjective experience, which takes place by turning inward.

This inward turn reveals the word *body* as a verb. Rather than a solid object little prone to change, we get to experience our body as a process. Our body is a site where multiple narratives, influences, identities, actions, and perceptions converge. We body time that is passing. We body space that is moving. Time and space also body us, that is moving, growing, aging, always in the process of change. We body feelings, ideas, and situations. To experience ourselves as a verb and experience its idle and thrust requires an inward turn, with us witnessing the changes from the front row of our attention.

Turning inward reveals a great unfolding of experiences that thinking traps with concepts and belief systems. Embodiment cares little about naming and conceptualizing. Embodiment knows flow, sensory awareness riding alongside shifting circumstances. For example, while typing these lines, I hear the neighbor's chain saw, feel it vibrate my temple, and wish it were not so loud; I sit cross-legged as I often do and elongate my spine a tad further, an adjustment of my position, which tends to tilt toward the computer the longer I write; I'm aware of the ease of my breath, my belly expanding with inhalations; I wonder how long my writing session will last today before I tire, the thought prompting my jaw to relax and my tongue to lift toward my upper palate; I hear the chain saw that fell quiet a second ago resume its buzz that oddly no longer annoys me; in ceasing typing, I notice clouds reflected on the computer screen and stare at nature appearing on my device, a reminder about activity taking place beyond the walls of my house. And so it goes, awareness spotlighting a parade of what is within sight, touch, proprioception, interoception, thought, and movement, an endless stream that is satisfying to focus on through writing because it grounds me in my body, free of any inclination to prove, impress, speculate, or conceptualize. Just notice. Another day, I may get up from my chair, turn on the music, and dance around the room. Either way, it's me engaging with what my senses detect. Were I to prolong the activity, my breath would deepen further, time would become elastic, and more details about my body and its engagement with surroundings would show up, my consciousness altered by this type of attention.

Turning attention inward connects us to the dynamic flux of our being. It's there we touch upon our individual somatic truths and its subjective, personalized experience of being. It's there we discover the value of coming home to our senses and our body. It's there that embodiment takes place. For a time, we can get by well enough ignoring our body, minus the essentials of eating, drinking, and sleeping, but at some point the body will request greater attention and the longer it is ignored, the more demanding it gets. Those who sleep too little, eat poorly, discount stress, and neglect self-care practices compromise their immune system and may end up temporarily bedridden while the body restores itself, its way of insisting on modifying behavior.

Among the most potent activities we can do is to pause during our hectic day to focus on breath and the senses. Consider it a mini staycation.

Try This

Turn off your phone, TV, computer, and iPod. Step into another room if that helps. Avoid distractions like taking the dog for a walk or responding to a call from family or a colleague. All in good time. Pause everything for two minutes. Luxuriate in stillness. Feel the weight of your body upon your seat. Feel your feet contacting your shoes and the floor. Notice how your clothes feel against your skin. Notice how your belly contracts and expands with each breath. Notice your lips, the nape of your neck, your jaw, your weariness, or excitability. Notice your parade of thoughts. Notice what you notice.

If you tried this activity, you know how difficult pausing can be. Likely your thoughts persisted in their relentless succession. Likely, too, you found out that requests upon your attention come from both outside, such as the notification buzz on our phone, and inside, the compulsion to read the notification or attend an itch. Each moment, a swarm of phenomena buzzes just outside the door of our attention—usually several doors—which we manage as best we can, all of which is done more easily with decent rest, nutrition, water, and self-care practices.

Pausing our usual activity and shifting attention to presence is vitalizing because it enables us to connect more authentically and viscerally with breath, thought, emotion, and feeling, essentially all the sizable and tiny building blocks that make us who we are moment to moment. We get to catch our breath. We feel the matter of our flesh. We reboot and restore. We hone in on what's important. The discoveries are endless.

Or we use the pause for simple motion like lifting and lowering the shoulders and doing it slowly as to engage muscles attentively, not automatically. There's a big difference. With the former, micromovements become perceptible and worlds unfold. Engaging the body in open intention reaps physical, emotional, intellectual, and energetic rewards. Movement reveals to what degree we inhabit or escape the home of our body. Its clues are everywhere, in our attention and inattention, in our flexibility and rigidness, in the depth and shallowness of our breath, in the dull or vibrant colors, tastes, and sounds we perceive, in our reluctance or fervor to express, in our habit of self-criticism or support. Our embodied world reveals its splendors.

Our body is the literal vehicle of our life and the metaphor for our relationship with existence. All that has taken place, every event and interaction, is imprinted upon our flesh, visible to those who read body cues and sensed by those who listen with muscles, organs, bones, hormones, cells, will, heart, mind, and energy. Dancer and founder of 5Rhythms, Gabrielle Roth, says the body "is your Bible, your encyclopedia, your life story. Everything that happens to you is stored and reflected in your body. Your body knows, your body tells.

The relationship of your self to your body is indivisible, inescapable, unavoidable."[14]

Movement brings impressions and stories to the surface and enables a flow with the flux of being. Sensing takes place. Coming home to our body takes place. Bodying takes place. Any movement stirs blood and heartbeat, reveals strain or ease, our body in sync with adaptability and the pulse of existence.

More so than many fitness regimes, dance provides potent exercise for the brain. Researchers discovered that the nonrepetitive movements of dance not only slow the aging brain but can reverse its deterioration. Researchers claim that "[D]ance training is superior to repetitive physical exercise in inducing brain plasticity in the elderly."[15] Other studies point out how dance improves motor coordination, especially helpful for people dealing with neurodegenerative diseases like Parkinson's, their tremors significantly subsiding.[16] British doctors have taken note and anticipate prescribing dance and other arts for ailments like dementia, psychosis, lung conditions, and anxiety.

Dancers need no convincing about the potency of movement. They savor physical expression, coordination, strength, and flexibility, the conscious and unconscious spoken through their moving body. They live choreographer Martha Graham's statement, "Dance is the hidden language of the soul."[17] Allowing and playing with the body's natural rhythms provides a visceral outlet of expression that reinforces innate intelligence and an effective path of learning.

INTEGRATION THROUGH EMBODIMENT

Healing, growth, and an experience of wholeness increase when we ground awareness in the body and move with intention. Movement expresses the mind, the mind is revealed through movement, and the brain's neuroplasticity creates routes for enlivening. Movement generates a feedback loop between body and mind, form and consciousness. Movement permits us to lose ourselves to motion only to find that much more of ourselves. We embody generative activity, life in constant motion.

Embodiment principles show up regularly in my writing, especially in my poetry, which is often a verbal dance, language moving through me like blood and pulse. Slowing down writing or speeding it up, depending on my recent habit, while turning attention to the body allows me to connect with each word and phrase as a somatic and syntactic event. In this approach, I discover language resonating in my flesh. Writing shows up as breath and energy made visible, meaning made meaningful, a moment's flux finding rhythmic expression and image on the line. Words have a reciprocal relationship with our flesh, enhancing perception, and awakening us to our inner world and its ties to the world beyond our body. The writing contributes to making sense of what is sensed, what lies in the shadows, and the impressions that flash into awareness like a lightning bug before blending back into the dark of night. The writing reflects and renders more perceptible the pulses and waves of our body, lines functioning as incantatory events letting us hear and, if wanted, to be heard by another, to see what may otherwise vanish with a blink.

The activity need not be writing or movement. Painting or singing, building code, or replacing the rotted floorboards on the porch can have a similar impact. The specific activity matters less than our approach to the activity. What is important is using it as an opportunity to attend to the senses.

Our relationship to our body is vital. It is our life vessel and temple, the site of feeling, thinking, and moving, where being takes place, where fields overlap, where the world beyond and within our skin intermingles. With embodiment, we discover we are not separate from experience, but its very manifestation. We are belly and belief, hands and hope, one who looks and one who is looked upon, one who is listening and one who speaks. Yet too many of us are overcritical, belittling, or disembodied. Surrounding commotion and inner chaos claim us as victim and we lose the ability to maintain an integrity of being and appreciate the multitude of sensory impressions. Our body, we believe, is not good enough, fit enough, smart enough, attractive enough, capable enough—an endless list of judgments that pushes us out of our body instead of dwelling as a welcome resident. Or we cherish it to a point of narcissism, devoting inordinate time and money on superficial enhancements that provide shine with little substance. Some people treat their car better than their body. How well we respect or dishonor our body, whether we regard it as an object to be manipulated and controlled or a valuable living form requiring care, carries over into how we treat our surroundings, be it our house or the Earth.

Our attitude toward our body can be the difference between health and disease. The tenor of our attitude, thoughts, and feelings impacts our cells. Biochemist Sondra Barrett refers to the antennae of cells, how the outer surface receptors of each cell listens to each other and responds to incoming information. Always on alert for danger, our cells will release the chemicals aiding us in flight or fight, the cells unable to make a difference between a real threat or an imagined one. She says, "Be aware that it's not simply physical events that trigger our "stress cocktails, our minds play an important role in our chemistry."[18]

Our cells are listening. Our heart and spleen are listening. Our blood and bones are listening. Our entire body is listening to what we think, say, and write, how we move and keep still, how we drive to work and answer the phone. We, this body, this mind and spirit, this energetic consciousness expressing self, is the plenitude of who we are, what we know about ourselves and the secrets yet to be revealed, the seed buried and the sprout breaking through the surface.

FIELD KNOWING

A key ingredient to embodied, integrative knowing and one regularly overlooked is the biofield. Granted, most of us have not been trained to perceive it so an initial step in knowing the field is acknowledging it exists.

This field contains a blueprint of our physical body and is the crossroads where we end and others begin. It contains vestiges of our thoughts and feelings along with the history and potential of our body. Energy practitioners commonly recognize the biofield as divided into four layers corresponding with us physically, mentally, emotionally, and spiritually, which interact with chakras, or energy centers, connected to main branches of the nervous system. Medical intuitive Dora Kunz saw its importance as "the transfer of life energy or vitality from the universal field to the individual field, and thence to the physical body. It is the primary contact with the ocean of life energy that sustains all of nature."[19] Energy healer Cyndi Dale sees the field serving "as collection and transmission centers for both subtle, or metaphysical, energy and concrete, or biophysical energy" that regulate our conscious and unconscious realities.[20] This blueprint is a valuable template for healing practitioners in determining blocked energy and restoring the flow essential to health. As science plays catch-up, researchers have begun to look at how the body emits biophotons, a naturally occurring light common among all living forms, and how the degree of light impacts health.[21]

Try This

Place your hands palm to palm facing each other with a few inches of space between them. What do you feel? Now rub them together for a few minutes and place them parallel to each other again. Slowly move them closer and farther apart. What do you detect? It's likely you'll experience heat, tingles, and a slight magnetic pull.

Try This

Extend your arms and slowly lift them upward. Imagine you are pushing through water. Spread the fingers to activate their sensors. Now slowly lower your arms. Repeat, pausing if there's strain. Eventually you'll feel a substance that is not quite water and not quite anything else that is familiar—your solid body extending itself electromagnetically and energetically beyond your skin.

Sensing the field that surrounds and permeates our body reveals us as more than a solid form. The body is also a field of electromagnetic and subtle energy, a composite of dynamic elements changing with every thought, feeling, and activity. With time, practice, and intention, any of us can learn to sense this field. Most of us already do—to a degree. Consider a time encountering a stranger and experiencing them as weighing us down or lifting us up. This is an example of feeling their field. Imagine what is possible when our attention is intentional and we practice expanding our perceptions. Ten-year-old Abigail, among my youngest clients, did not need practice. Her mother brought her to me because two years of doctor's visits made no improvement to incessant headaches and eye floaters brought on by a concussion. From the first session, Abigail giggled every time my hands moved around her body. She felt tickling tingles and was especially soothed when my hands hovered near her head. She felt the warmth of my body even when I stood a few feet away. After two sessions, her headaches disappeared and the floaters shrank by 75 percent.

Now, as mentioned earlier in this chapter, I'll share the story that continues to amaze me and raises questions as to what else is possible upon opening perceptual doors. When the world went into COVID lockdown and urged six feet of social distancing, my energy healing practice suddenly became hazardous and I canceled my appointments, lest my clients or I inadvertently infect each other. Nevertheless, the prospect of reduced income panicked me. After a few days of long walks, I recalled an incident with Joe from a few years earlier. Joe lived a two-hour drive away and reached out to me about his appendix surgery. Postsurgery, the doctor announced all was well, the inflamed pouch removed, yet my friend's abdominal pain not only persisted but was increasing. "Can you work on me?" he pleaded by phone.

"Can you drive here?" I replied.

Commonly clients sit on the couch or chair in my space, where we talk about their condition. Then they remove their shoes, belt, and eyeglasses before getting on the massage table. I move around the table, my hands alternating between resting on and hovering a few inches away from their body to further assess their condition and implement a technique.

That's not what he had in mind. He wanted a distant healing session. His body would not cross the threshold of my door, let alone get onto the massage table for my hands to pass over or land upon his body.

Highways, bridges, traffic lights, shopping malls, high rises, subdivisions, cell phone towers, electric poles, computers on desks and computers on laps, friends drinking coffee, friends taking a walk, friends proposing more than a friendship, pets on their leash and pets running freely in parks, these and a crowd of other familiar signs of contemporary life lie between us. As did my cynicism, wedged between us like a concrete highway wall built to soundproof neighborhoods. Out of friendship and concern, I agreed to try—emphasis on try—with little faith in my ability. It's one thing for flesh to meet flesh and the field of our heat and the subtle and electromagnetic energy to mingle, but crossing the miles was another matter altogether.

After the session, we spoke. To my surprise, the pain vanished and hadn't recurred when we chatted again a week later. A coincidence with a happy ending, I surmised, my cynic glad to reinforce a limited belief system. I didn't think about the event again until panicking at the possibility of not being able to pay my bills set in.

Just try, I thought. I texted a client struggling with asthma and depression resulting from the sudden death of his son.

"Give it a try," I suggested, confident that the only potential harm would be to my ego. He agreed and I moved around the table to work on his body, except his was an imagined body. My hands feeling into the empty space above the massage table encountered neither flesh nor hair.

We spoke on the phone afterward. "That was fabulous," he said. "I feel great! How did you do that?" he asked.

"What happened?" I asked as surprised as he.

I reached out to other clients for trial runs and each reported results similar to what takes place in person: pain levels diminish, sinuses clear, migraines vanish, anxiety lowers, trembles cease. Additionally, my hands would heat up, as often happens in person, and I was able to see into their body. Something wholly unfamiliar and mysterious was taking place and continues to seize my curiosity.

With repeated successes with clients a few or hundreds of miles away from my healing table, I now recognize that proximity doesn't matter, that it's not necessary we be in the same room nor, at times, to use my hands—I imagine my hands moving instead. What is required is focusing on their body with my expanded senses. With my senses heightened, information that typically comes through my hands arrives through intuition or another available channel.

My attempt to explain how this invisible, far-reaching circuitry works leaves me faltering for words. In that, I'm not alone. Physician and researcher Daniel Benor acknowledges distant healing's effectiveness, but like other researchers, does not understand the mechanism that makes it effective. Having reviewed over sixty studies of distant healing, he states, "The issues raised by distant healing research are extremely complex. [It] is truly at the frontiers of science in exploring these borderlands between Newtonian and quantum worlds, between the realms of matter and of spirit, through the study of subtle energies and energy medicine."[22]

A colleague in engineering and physics who I met during a conference held on Zoom might point to this quantum world as well. We exchanged email addresses in the chat before her name disappeared from the session. Her email arrived a day later along with an explanation for her departure. "Attending the conference, but also meeting with students, researching for a paper, then popping into another Zoom session," she explained, and then the line that set my mind ablaze: "I was like a quantum particle or wave, being in multiple places simultaneously." She was obviously referring to her pandemic multitasking where prongs of her attention plugged into multiple cities across the globe with a few taps of the keyboard for conversations with colleagues, an activity a nineteenth-century mind would deem impossible. Her comment made me realize I was experiencing my quantum self, my attention and perceptions occupying two places at once, no internet connection needed.

Distant healing supports physician Larry Dossey's idea of non-locality, that consciousness is not limited by the borders of the physical body. He suggests that consciousness transcends our skin. He says, "Minds, rather, are nonlocal with respect to space and time. This means that the separateness of minds is an illusion, because individual minds cannot be put in a box (or brain) and walled off from one another."[23]

Newtonian physics considers the body mechanistically as a collection of functional parts, the brain often referred to as a computer, but healers like Barbara Brennan recognize our matter as fluid and dynamic. She says, "The whole universe appears as a dynamic web of inseparable energy patterns. . . . Thus we are not separated parts of a whole."[24]

What is this whole? It depends on how you define the body. As blood, bones, and breath. As a mobile, watery sack. As a house for our feelings, sensations, and thoughts. As electromagnetic pulses. As atoms, vibration, and spirit. As a field of energy. As a living form that enables me to write these words and you to read them.

Most of us go about our day without consciously sensing our quantum self or the biofield, our cultural filters blind to such a perception. It's not the case in places like Hong Kong, where strangers have come up to me to comment on the colors in my field with the same casualness that an American may comment on my dress. By turning attention toward the biofield, we can access a trove of information, our experience of embodiment expanded to include our energetic self. It is a useful and critical reminder—our body is part of a much larger body. The perception is beneficial in knowing that we can support others near and far. It is comforting to realize we are not as alone as we may think we are. It is helpful information for highly sensitive individuals who readily absorb the feelings of others and have difficulty maintaining their centeredness as happened with Claire, who came to me complaining about exhaustion, anxiety, and a mix of emotions, including sadness and anger, for which she didn't know the cause. My exploration of her field revealed these emotions not as hers, but her coworkers'—she was soaking up their feelings like a towel in water. We worked on grounding her energy and developing field hygiene, a procedure for clearing her field of the unwelcome residue that disturbed her balance. I showed her how to take an energetic shower and move the residue away from her. Practicing field hygiene enables us to function as optimally as possible and clear up the thoughts, feelings, and sensations that can throw us off-kilter. Practicing field hygiene keeps psychic germs and interference away. To practice field hygiene, it is helpful to learn to sense or at minimum to believe in the existence of our field.

Believing the field exists and experiencing it may position us at an edge of understanding, of perception, and consciousness. Here exists the dance of us and not us, the story written and the story as yet unwritten. Here are a me and a we awaiting growth and a new type of knowing. It's up to each of us to appreciate the presence of the field, to use it to deepen our relationship with self, and to find a way to integrate it into the fullness of who we are. What our body once knew may no longer hold true, or only partly, its hunger summoning us to the frontier.

Despite my many experiences with the field and healing, my intent is not to convince you about its existence. Okay, maybe a little. But convincing suggests imposing my ideas on you and implying that you experience it the same way. We may experience similarities, but the path to embodiment and knowing is through your own firsthand experiences. Yes, I'm pointing out a region for which you may have little experience. Notably, my preference is toward respecting, uplifting, and opening your mind to details in the landscape that you may have overlooked. Rest in the grounded stillness of your body and reach out little by little. Talk to others. Read. Take a class. Keep a notebook of your findings. Considering its possibility opens the senses wider than is customary. What this new sensing is likely to reveal are the blocks and the unblocking of new ways to perceive your body and the way forward on your evolutionary path.

4

The Ecology of the Self

I like to define biology as the history of the Earth and all its life—past, present, and future. To understand biology is to understand that all life is linked to the earth from which it came; it is to understand that the stream of life, flowing out of the dim past into the uncertain future, is in reality a unified force, though composed of an infinite number and variety of separate lives.

RACHEL CARSON

During one of my short breaks from writing, I walked the modest path meandering through my backyard and viewed the young dogwood tree with its first-ever pink blooms, a sure sign of recuperating from a bout of fungus. Nearby, emboldened violets fill the interior of the fire pit. Each year furthers the transformation of this small plot of land into a refuge for bees, bats, and birds, pluckings for salad, inspiration for creative work and healing, and a space for meditation. When I pour compost-rich water onto the tomatoes, cucumbers, peppers, basil, and cilantro, a part of me enlivens as if my own chlorophyll bathes in the sunlight.

A close look at the leaves reveals their venation, reticulated, palmate, or parallel, unfurling or spreading, their particular shade of green best identified by naming the plant. I lean in to peer at the ferns, hostas, and rhododendrons as if to hear secrets they may impart. But it's not words I seek during these garden respites but a marveling and connecting with nature and beauty. Regardless of whether the sun is high in the sky, the moon peers down between branches, or the yard is shrouded by fog, beauty awaits the dilation of my pupils, my heart and attention tuned to nature's changes. Ecopsychologist Laura Sewall would suggest that the textured, sensual details of nature have awakened my senses and neural network, furthering perception.

Shape and color delay my return to pending work. Or it's the wind swaying a stem or a ladybug hiking across a leaf. These are the siren calls that disrupt my usual preoccupations. I am summoned to witness and tower above them like a giant careful not to crush these delicate forms with an inattentive step. They are reminders of resilience, an intimate call to my own nature, and a marveling at how life unfolds. We grow alongside each other. We journey out from the earth. Witnessing feels like a high calling and an opening that returns me to the home of my body.

A similar summons occurs when I gaze upon an infant. We share a field of curiosity and love. In that invitational space, I've no disagreements with life, no need to assert a claim, no need to do anything other than align with what is taking place and breathe in the awe of homecoming.

I would hope most of us have experienced a similar exquisite connection with a beloved, be it a family member, pet, or plant, the separateness of our life expanded by another's presence, the heart pulsing in a quiet ecstasy. Such unity waters and fertilizes being. The connection amplifies the breath and breadth of who we are and reinforces a sense of belonging that includes our achievements as well as our imperfections and unfinished tasks. What takes place is experiencing inclusion in something larger than our limiting ego often wrangling for top place. Turning away from a vibrant connection feels like a violation of natural

laws, an existential fall, a violence against being, the delusion of an iso-
late, a symptom of toxic individualism. Instead, there is only one wise
choice, turning toward. Turning toward is to join a consciousness larger
than our singular worries, despairs, and hopes. We get to whisper with
the wind, follow the flight of a hummingbird, or sit beneath the maple
tree. The process assigns us membership into a club whose doors remain
open, no forms or background check needed. Just us, as is, no references
needed.

This joyful connecting, like a ripe peach for the soul, happens
also with art, poetry, music, and dance, among the reasons many of us
agree to practice them or be their audience. A brush stroke, a verbal
phrase, the reach of an outstretched arm, or a vibrato filling a room
quickens the heart, activates mirror neurons, and alters consciousness.
Who we were a moment ago shifts. Thoughts usually jostling for position settle down. The heart steadies into an easy, wondrous beat. As if
lights turned off in one part of the room illuminate the entire house,
as if pain dissolves into relief, as if exile from a tribe ends with a feast
for tongue, ears, heart, and soul, as if every precious moment, every
trial, hope, and aspiration was preparation for this moment, which is
perfect.

The beauty is unmistakable. Over here, it says, and gladly we go
to receive its gifts. Imagine the mosaic ceiling of a chapel or mosque
or the jeweled torso of a beetle. Recall the shudder when a warm
voice and a gentle hand upon our arm melted the freeze of our heart
and rekindled the glow of love. Recall the resplendent harmony and
compulsive beat of music. Attention broadens and the mind opens
to a design of grandeur, a shift that is humbling and awe inspiring. Beauty is a portal to an expanded consciousness and irrefutable
splendor. Psychologist James Hillman recognizes beauty as "the way
in which the Gods touch our senses, reach the heart and attract us
into life."[1]

The call to practice art, poetry, music, or dance is an opportunity to engage beauty in its creative flow that is unconditionally welcoming and resonant. Just be. Just express. Creativity embraces our idiosyncratic rhythms, our hesitations and alacrity, our sloppiness and grace, our saying, seeing, and motion, the boundaries of a self edging inward and outward simultaneously. We touch into the intimacy of our body and the region larger than our usual sensing. We stir the cauldron of the unconscious toward consciousness. A creative practice puts us in dialogue with nature, with integration, with the unfolding of order and chaos. Any medium works when we alternate control with letting go, soliciting form with being informed, when we engage imaginally, inviting a dreamlike awareness and a furthering of cognitive awareness. Deep satisfaction arises from riding the waves of expression, one word or image or note offering its hand to the next, one gesture spilling into the next, a flow state that connects into a field that is affirming, inspiring, and generative.

THE PRESENCE OF BEAUTY

Experiences of beauty, be it with nature, art, or a beloved, situate us in the thick of life as an integral player who has pursued or lucked into a moment of connection. I wish an experience of beauty upon everyone. Such connections recalibrate temperament and shift brain chemistry to release dopamine and oxytocin, hormones that reinforce joy and a sense of belonging. Such connections renew our sense of purpose and authenticity. The connection reduces stress, the harbinger of so many illnesses. Instead, all systems shift toward balance, us situated in contentment crowned by an acceptance of all that is. This deep connection, no part of us exiled is, I believe, what most of us want. Says poet Derek Wolcott, "Give back your heart/ to itself, to the stranger who has loved you/ all your life, whom you ignored."[2] Welcome to the bliss of an evolutionary shift. Welcome to a more complete you. Welcome to the home of your body that includes your place in the world.

Try This

Recall an event with a beloved. It could be a partner, child, pet, a piece of art, or an uplifting setting in nature. Recall the warmth and ease the experience generated. Invite the memory of the feeling back into your heart. Place your hand at the center of your chest. Let the recalled feelings well up. Let them radiate throughout your entire body to the tips of your fingers and toes. Enjoy the warming expansiveness and whatever else you notice.

A sense of belonging provides us with the resilience to handle what the day offers, able to greet each request and demand upon our attention with equanimity. The power of love, beauty, and harmony carries us in a current that matches and fortifies our strength, dissolving habits that do not have our best interests at heart. The music of a fern is our music. The grace of a dancer is our grace. The eyes that look with love are love itself. It is our due and our doing for partaking in community, the me with you with everything and everyone else.

If we feel cut off, isolated, lonely, or alienated, it may be a result of where we habitually situate our gaze, the trauma, tensions, and emotions held in the body, the thoughts we entertain, the activities we choose, the filters employed. We may have subscribed to a paradigm of separation, our ego in competition with others, an "us vs. them" mentality, a belief that we are not good enough as is and we need to demonstrate our worth and superiority. We end up at odds with ourselves and our surroundings, crippled by polarization. The repercussion of this pattern is to lock us in and apart, connection severed, our health and well-being compromised.

Aware that mental health issues are one of the most rapidly increasing causes of long-term sick leave, the insurance company Cigna released a report that revealed that adults between the ages of twenty-three and thirty-seven are lonelier and in worse health than previous generations.[3]

Cigna places the blame on the lack of in-person contact and the hours spent with electronic screens, the need for social distancing during the COVID pandemic intensifying that loneliness. Missing is reaching across the illusion of our division. Missing is connecting within to the mosaic of our inner self. Missing is going out in nature, which touches into our sensuality.

A study by Seattle Children's Research Institute found that children spend as little as two hours outdoors a week, adults placing them instead in artificial environments.[4] The lack of outdoor activity impacts the development of sensory and motor skills and prevents children from getting sufficient vitamin D, a weakening of their inner ecology. What gets sacrificed is exposure and engagement with nature's rhythms and advancing sensory intelligence. What gets sacrificed is experiencing a visceral connection to their body. Missing is enjoying the countless experiences that a grounded body provides. Even a short walk on a city sidewalk can reinforce the nature within and transform a weakness into a strength, a disconnection into a reminder of beauty.

Establishing and increasing connection can start with something as simple as a sigh, our body invited to sip from the simplicity of sensory attention. Shoulders hike up and lower and coincide with expelling air from our lungs. Experiencing the felt present moment loosens the tendency to quickly translate experience and shirk embodiment. Instead, with our story as yet untold, tensions release, walls crumble, and restless thoughts can settle. In extending a breath practice or pursuing another embodiment activity, we discover that we are no more alone than a bee in a hive or a car on a highway. If it appears otherwise, it's likely due to a habit of our focus. Instead we look up and look out. We feel within. We extend the reach of sensing. Try another perspective. Any attempt brings us closer. An experience of connection and wholeness awaits.

If uncomfortable feelings show up as they are wont to do, we acknowledge them like a difficult friend. Sit and breathe with them. Or express them through movement, drawing, or another chosen medium.

Relief eventually comes with attention and intention, time and practice. The same holds true for feelings tied to trauma and the belief that the original unpleasant or horrific event is stitched into the flesh permanently. Debilitating pain can feel as if it has set up permanent residency within and refuses to exit despite our pleas. It does dissipate—with time, compassion, determination, and the right combination of practices. If doing so alone feels daunting or unmanageable, a professional can assist in dissolving the stitches and getting past seemingly insurmountable hurdles. The peace that is our birthright is as close as a breath away.

At thirty-two years old, Kaylen came to me with a lengthy list of acute physical and emotional ailments and was leaning toward quitting work and going on disability, which she preferred not to do. She could barely get through the day without intense pain, fatigue, and despair resulting from childhood sexual abuse and teen date rape. Her body was a sheath of armor, her stiff shoulders concave around her chest, her breath shallow. She believed minimizing movement provided safety. The reverse was true, however. The constant muscle strain contributed to exhaustion and ongoing pain. Our work together softened the hardened sheath of her flesh until it became more like frayed, worn cloth, and eventually her chronic pains vanished. With several of her symptoms gone, others dramatically lessened; she lowered the dosage and stopped taking some medications and was able to resume work more energized and upbeat than she'd felt in years.

THE FEAR PARADIGM

Among the messages broadcast culturally is fear. From a young age we are taught to be wary of the ill-intended stranger. This stranger could be a person who lives next door, across town, from another state or country, essentially anyone unknown, unfamiliar, and seemingly unlike us. We are not taught to assess each person individually, appreciate differences, nor develop the valuable skill of determining who to avoid and who to trust. This fear, when left unexamined, reinforces anxiety and social isolation. Further neglect establishes a foundation for xenophobia and racism, our inability to connect projected as disregard, even hatred toward another.

Adding to the potpourri of fear is news transmitted through a variety of electronic devices that feed us a constant diet of frightful stories about killings, rape, theft, corruption, disease, floods, wildfires, climate emergencies, and much more than I care to list. The language employed to tell these social, political, and medical stories is often rife with violent metaphors. The metaphors effectively seize our attention. They also unsettle our nervous system. We are "at war" with poverty, drugs, and terrorism. There's a war on women, masculinity, Christmas, and democracy. We "fight" cancer and continually look for "smoking guns." Ad agencies, marketers, and newspapers know that fear sells, that "if it bleeds, it leads." More than catchy phrases, they reinforce a perception of dangers lurking everywhere. The perception initiates the fight-or-flight response, the release of cortisol, a neurological pattern forming, the body on edge as it looks out for and expects the enemy. Believing the story and subscribing to the paradigm leads to finding the evidence that supports a fearful belief, a bias activated, our serenity invaded as collateral damage. It becomes hard to focus on work, to attend to our families, and to sleep through the night without terror disrupting our rest.

I don't mean to minimize perils. It's good to know about real dangers in order to avoid them and alter the policies and behaviors that created them. It's beneficial to know the source of *E. coli,* the impact of pesticide exposure, the link between corporate greed, climate destruction, and the urgency to lower our carbon footprint. It's essential to learn how to minimize the spread of a virus. Information enables us to make wise and informed decisions toward altering behaviors. Information enables us to engage in appropriate actions. However, the problem with the message of fear is its pervasiveness and how it eclipses alternatives and solutions. We become the deer in the headlights unable to leap to safety.

The message spills into multiple areas of our lives. We fear losing our jobs, our health, our money, our loved ones, our homes. We fear walking alone at night, leaving the door unlocked, switching jobs, growing up or old, and making a decision. We fear the farming practices of our food, the material in our clothes, and the substances in our electronic gear. The hazards are everywhere, and our ability to discern between real and imagined hazards becomes blurred. As a result, our productivity, health, compassion, and ease are negatively impacted. The range of our sensory experiences retreats and abilities atrophy.

Fear is experienced not as a subjective perspective, one of many possible responses, but as Truth itself, a prevailing attitude that clouds everything. Unable to see the complexity of situations and people, we mistake fear not as a perspective or a response to a specific situation but as a realistic appraisal. Rather than helping, the fear filter hurts us. We feel unsafe to be ourselves, on guard, always on the lookout for the situation or person who will rob us of all that we hold dear. The fear perspective reinforces a scarcity mentality that justifies the need to hold back and hold on to because needed goods, be they emotional or physical, are in short supply. A part of us shuts down. It's a dog-eat-dog world and only the strongest survive, we believe, which justifies Othering and any harm inflicted upon another.

Too much fear leads to despair and resignation. We see no point in acting since the feared results seem imminent. Journalist Mike Pearl refers to the impact of climate despair by citing a study in which research subjects "were urged, in fear-based terms, to take action or else . . . if you tell people something must be done or we're all gonna' die, they tend to take door number two, however irrational that impulse may seem."[5] Dare we believe that a singular action or a group of committed people can turn a negative situation around to our betterment, that our salvation and thriving is achievable? Dare we have faith in our own abilities and form a coalition of the resilient and resourceful? Dare we invest and trust in our imagination?

The fear perspective, or paradigm, may be more problematic than is realized. Among the problems with fear is how our bodies react to chronically elevated levels of stress, rendering our perception of potential hazards as similar or more dangerous than the hazards themselves. Living with a steady diet of fear seriously degrades our health. Fear can weaken the immune system, disrupt hormone production, and cause cardiovascular damage. It can impair formation of long-term memories and areas of the brain, such as the hippocampus, which can leave us chronically anxious. Long-term consequences of elevated fear include fatigue, depression, anxiety, and PSTD. The Anxiety and Depression Association of America states that forty million adults in the United States age eighteen and older, 18.1 percent of the population, suffer from anxiety disorders, with women twice as likely to suffer as men.[6] Those numbers show no sign of going down any time soon.

It's likely that we do not recall signing on the dotted line for a subscription to the fear paradigm, nor do we recognize the symptoms as anything out of the ordinary. It can be hard to shift from autopilot to awareness, from subscription to a cultural belief system into the truth of our own personal experience, from somatic and energetic illiteracy to somatic and energetic intelligence, from despair to empowerment. Besides, we say with an uneasy chuckle, who isn't anxious these days?

We do ourselves a favor by considering other paradigms and questioning any that may be operating by default in the background. A shift in perspective supports the resilience of our body to focus on a more generous and generative expression that welcomes health and growth. A shift readies us to find solutions to intransigent problems and engage in practices that support the complexity of our nature. A shift recognizes challenges, even seemingly intractable ones, as opportunities.

In the spirit of balance, presence, health, and a habitable future, I propose an alternative to fear. I propose love.

Love, like beauty, places us in harmony with ourselves. It is the brilliant light in the dark, energy lush in its flow, and the spirit situated in its rightful place. Love's nectar courses through the body, an energy that supports us rising into and embodying our potential. The warmth and radiance of its current feels like the reason for existence itself. With love, everything falls into place and coherence. It's not that we've met the person of our dreams, been given a new car, found that methane disappeared, and discovered the ills of the world magically went away. Rather, the factors previously contributing to stress and dismay now feel manageable as part of love's unfolding, each moment perfect in its imperfections. We feel limitless and free to expose our subtle, tender, and glistening truths. We feel ready to confront what shows up, silently cheered on by rain, gravity, and a friend miles away. Love reveals us as a body in process, a living form in dialogue with breath, motion, sun, and all that surrounds us.

THE PERVASIVENESS OF LOVE

Love is a radiating center that supports health, opening, and interconnection. We feel at ease with ourselves and others. When we listen to the wise counsel of our heart, it contributes to collaborative action because it knows we are inseparable from one another, that what falls upon you also falls upon me, visible in areas like the web of the economy, health care, and the environment. Which is why unfastening the heart's door can feel so overwhelming, our immediate family not only immediate, but also reaching across a cacophony of space. It reminds us to listen to the flapping wings of birds or the prayer of a stone. It gets us to hear the voice of the wind and the song of the earth. It offers a remedy to a pain tied to our longing and growth and reminds us, too, about this paradisiacal moment.

For every emotion, there is a physical and energetic correspondence, a pattern that appears in our fascia and cells, our mood and motivation, and a shift in one area impacts another. From a mechanistic perspective, the body is a collection of parts as if each arm, leg, and hip joint exists in isolation. Surgery reinforces that idea with its ability to replace a damaged part with a prosthetic, a metal and plastic combination taking the place of a worn knee, for instance. From an integrative perspective, our so-called parts are a combination of overlapping physical, chemical, and energetic matter. Touch or move one area of the body and we touch and move the entirety of our being. Get hired for a new job and hope blooms. Vacation at the mountains and watch the sun rise above the grid of our thoughts. Experience the uplift of love and the entire body rises to the occasion.

A preliminary assessment I perform with my clients is to feel their field and determine how far it extends from their body. Although the field may not be consistent, heat or density appearing in one location only, for instance, or its egg-like shape full of irregularities such as a protrusion or hole, I've come to recognize three basic patterns: fields extending from the body little more than an inch; fields extending a few inches; and fields extending several inches or a few feet. Those with the smallest, densest fields tend to be anxious, angry, bitter, and untrusting. They suffer from various chronic and acute physical and emotional ailments. Their outermost field is murky and uneven. In contrast, those with the biggest fields are largely content and optimistic, their outer field translucent. The latter group may seek treatment for temporary issues like a sprained or broken bone, rehabilitation from surgery, mild anxiety, or a desire for a life change. Interestingly, if the individuals with the smaller fields imagine a loving friend, pet, or family member, their field quickly brightens and extends.

Fear prompts the body to contract and withdraw while love encourages expansion and connection. The body responds well to love. Love reduces or eliminates the negative impact of stress, strengthens the immune system, and supports hormonal balance. Love is generative, generous, resilient, resourceful, and creative. Love provides the strength and courage to look difficulties in the face and find ways to resolve them. Instead of harping on what's wrong with a situation, love enables us to cultivate what is beneficial. Here's a noteworthy difference: whereas fear controls us, making us victim to harrowing circumstances, love supports making choices with us taking charge. The latter leads to us being responsive, empowered, and resilient. We are active participants, supporters, and eventual victors, all of which contributes to making constructive decisions. If the results don't work out as well as hoped, we adapt with an eye toward modification and improvement. With choice comes freedom and enlivening, the warmth of compassion and confidence permeating the body and radiating outward.

The choice to engage love is pivotal. It's not a matter of waiting for a beloved to show up or circumstances to change, a passive act that could, as my single friends looking for a partner admit, take eons to fulfill. It does mean choosing resilience, growth, wholeness, and transformation. It means tossing the baggage and clutter of our life, performing a mental, emotional, spiritual, and energetic spring cleaning, and opening to the fresh air and renewal of new perspectives. It means forgiving shortcomings in ourselves and others regarding hopes, expectations, and any intended or unintended harm. It means framing setbacks and obstacles as opportunities, the story not done until reaching a heartened chapter, a lesson learned, a transformation activated, a balance claimed. It means stepping fully into and trusting the completeness of our nature. It means recognizing the pervasiveness of beauty in the scent of lavender, in the design of a chair, in the stain in the carpet, in the ache in our heart, in the return of a tumor, in a worry and relief about tomorrow. It means recognizing connection everywhere in everyone and everything, that an animating force filtering through every part of life awaits our attention, a winding path engaging presence essential to our journey of wholeness. It means there's no better time or situation than here and now.

The choice to engage love is a revolutionary shift. It's not only mystics and futurists who urge its embrace but also medical practitioners recognizing the deleterious impact of chronic stress, positive psychologists focusing on what makes us thrive—essentially any of us who choose to smile at the morning's light and not pull the blanket over our eyes. Yet the cynics among us give love a bad rap. Best to keep love to pop songs and fruity New Agers. The cynic is alive and well among those jaded by a series of disappointments and intellectuals trained to poke holes in the weakness of an argument. There's great benefit to challenging logic and the status quo, especially if the aim is to improve and develop an idea. It's problematic, however, when it's a knee-jerk response that includes living from the head and habit to the exclusion of the rest of the body, a sure route to disembodiment and depreciation of new information. Love can also get sidelined because a show of emotion may be considered a weakness, emotion associated and disparaged as feminine, yet another example of misogyny on display.

My cynic rears its head at signs of a saccharine love that asks no questions and lacks depth. I cringe at the overeager jumping onto the love bandwagon singing its praise songs and indulging in hugs and feel-good celebrations without honest self-examination. Ignorance comes in many forms, as an overzealous lover and a rambunctious warrior. Both have rushed to judgment, eager to join a group or ideal without first establishing the balance that genuine love provides.

The love promoted here is mature and based on the waves of sensation associated with heart awareness. It listens, supports, and asserts. It is integrative, vitalizing, and encouraging. The root of *encourage,* from the Old French word *encoragier,* means "to make strong or hearten." Living from the heart, where love is sourced, provides the strength and ability to grow into conscious embodiment, into the fullness of our potential, into our being and becoming. With love, the heart hardened by disappointments and hurts softens and swells, responsive to what is present, in touch with new events, thoughts, and sensation. Its powerful electrical and bioenergetic current unites with other currents in the body, particularly the head and gut powerhouses, and sends its waves beyond the body. Interestingly, the symbol associated with the heart in the chakra systems is two triangles, one inverted, understood as the intersection between the physical (lower) and the spiritual (upper) body, the union of the feminine with the masculine, reason in balance with emotion. As a transit hub, the heart plays a vital role in engaging with what matters most and is a key player as a catalyst for change.

Engaging love is not carte blanche to act on every whim because what feels good has got to be good. It's not all heart and no brain, but the body working as a whole. It's heart and mind and awareness. It's expression and reflection. It's looking inward and outward and feeling the corresponding waves. Engaging the heart and feeling its warm, pulsing glow relaxes us into the strength and softness of our being, into bodying and a heightening of consciousness.

MATURITY OF THE HEART

Mature love taps into wisdom and inspiration. It anchors input from the heart, mind, and body as equal partners. These precious resources support making healthy choices in food, activity, thought, work, relationships, interactions, community, spiritual practice, and environmental actions. It supports learning to love our entire being, including what's most shameful. Anything less than total acceptance is a violence toward self. We love our achievements, health, talents, and our inner and outer beauty. We also love our imperfections, losses, limitations, pains, sickness, mistakes, and misshapen body. All of it. Not just what's easy to love: our toned body, an adorable pet, our thriving garden, our recent promotion, our low cholesterol numbers. We unsubscribe from self-criticism, which is a culturally sanctioned behavior—misery may love company but it's not the best company—and choose a more wholesome and integrative perspective that respects all of life, idiosyncrasies and anomalies included, improving upon what may need improvement yet without an emotional hook. We welcome What Is.

Mature love does not need to rely on an idealization to fill in for lapses. Mature love has no need to create fantasies, however tempting they may be. No if-only's: if only we were at the beach, if only we were more secure, attractive, or intelligent or whatever other quality appeals. These pose as potential traps that contribute to stress and imbalance. They create obstacles to being present, disconnect us from our body, and keep us from what is most helpful at the moment. Instead love is based on realistic and honest appraisals. We accept What Is this moment with all its sundry appearances. We feel without resistance. We reflect and remain open. We practice self-care, set boundaries, and respect limitations. We listen for the wisdom of the body in whatever channel it comes through. We mine daydreams for insight and inspiration. We go for a bike ride or sit on the porch. We immerse our foot into the stream of being. When necessary and the time is right, we make a change. We learn when going with the flow is appropriate and when waiting is a better strategy. Among our most vital practices is being present with What Is.

The heart, responsible for pumping blood, supplying oxygen and nutrients to the tissues, and removing wastes like carbon dioxide, is anchor and boat, filament and light, source and resource. It centers us within and connects us with what lies beyond the skin. It puts us in coherence with ourselves and in sympathetic resonance with everything else. Our feel-good system is activated, the brain releasing endorphin, oxytocin, serotonin, and dopamine.

With the heart engaged, hormones and nervous system in balance, we are better able to discern situations that uplift rather than degrade our energy. It's the compass that provides useful feedback as to when we're on course and when we've strayed. Its intuitive guidance steers us toward effectively dealing with whatever situation or person shows up, determining which of our resources to draw from and when to seek additional help.

Once we've subscribed to love, the signs start showing up: the stranger on the sidewalk smiling at us, the fellow shopper at the grocery store who offers to assist us when we struggle to reach the sparkling water tucked back on the top shelf, a realization that the work we have done today is good enough even though we haven't checked off all on our to-do list. We feel motivated and upbeat about tomorrow. There's an uptick in our energy, attitude, and outlook. Yes, it's a perspective with its own inherent bias but when done with eyes open, its particular intelligence supports balance and a breadth of information, our best interests, allowing us to rest in the grace of our wholeness. The body's chemistry flows, no system overly taxed.

INTERCONNECTION

We are more alike than different and more affiliated with nature than apart. "Every atom that belongs to me also belongs to you," says Walt Whitman.[7] If we experience a disconnect from love, beauty, or nature, it's likely the result of being disconnected from our own nature, from our body, from our energetic field, from our integrated intelligence, and our ability to experience the continuum of reaching within and beyond ourselves. We share bacteria, DNA, matter, water, and oxygen. We share thoughts, emotions, and belief systems. We share in the ideas of our family, job, city, and country. One's thoughts and actions, be it from a person or group, impact another's thoughts and actions, showing up in our body, speech, and mind. Your chain saw disturbs my peace. My peace reinforces your peace. Your building skills construct a new bookshelf for me to remove piles of books off the floor of my office. My reduced clutter lowers my stress and enables me to meet with clients and students with greater ease. My ease contributes to enabling them to go about their lives with more support and fewer complications. The cascade of interlinked events is endless like a tree whose visible and unseen roots extend beyond a single plot of land.

Sometimes it takes a dramatic event to reveal the power of such a network. On his way to a dance retreat, Andrew fell asleep at the wheel and collided head on with a tractor trailer, metal puncturing organs and breaking bones. Already at the retreat, I was among the dozens told he may not survive and participated in an impromptu, impassioned circle of prayers and chants. Over the days and weeks while he slipped in and out of consciousness, friends, family, and colleagues showed up at his bedside to sing and dance, those further away sending messages for a full convalescence. He survived the accident albeit with months of rehabilitation and extensive scarring and realized the importance of a supportive community whose well wishes he felt even when unconscious. He later wrote, "[S]o many were willing to pour out their love to me. . . . there for each of us. I wonder why it takes such a near-tragic event to stimulate and solidify the ever-present community that holds us."[8]

Another's feelings impact us in ways we may not realize. In the car on my way to a gathering for a retreat at the beach, I sat in the back seat excited about our proximity to the ocean and anticipated discussions about health, creative expression, and spirituality. As soon as I walked through the door, my mood quickly dimmed and my thoughts became a surprisingly disturbed stream of petty criticisms about the curtains, the floor, and the clothing of my colleagues. Spurts of criticism have happened before when I've stayed up too late and my tired body needs sleep, a warning I since heed to not put off bed, but this was midday, and I was well rested and excited. For the next few hours I struggled to understand what prompted the vitriol. That evening, the group gathered for introductions and the last women to speak said, "I've been hesitant to bring this up all afternoon but . . ." She admitted to fears of other's criticisms about the space, her dress, a lengthy list that coincided with mine. As she spoke and owned her feelings, my criticalness disappeared as if the mercury in a thermometer plummeted from fever to a normal temperature. Not only had she projected her feelings onto us, but I also became their unwitting container, a reminder about the need to regularly ground myself. What if I had been more reactive to the feelings when they first arrived? How often do we take on another's feelings without awareness? Upon entering an empty room, how often do we pick up on the residue of feelings from previous activities and occupants?

We are held, the network more intricate that we realize. We are part of an incomprehensibly vast, interconnected web of life, a cog in the ecosystem, a speck of life and citizen of the planet and universe. We are breath and afterthought, the food previously placed on our plate, and waves of measurable and unmeasurable interdependent energy. Our body is the meeting place of every person and ideology encountered, an energetic field intersecting innumerable other fields of people, animals, plants, insects, and minerals forming an inexplicable and illimitable field of life. Ancient Buddhist texts refer to this vast interconnection of phenomenon as Indra's Net, "an imperial net of celestial jewels extending in all directions infinitely, without limit."[9]

From the perspective of quantum physics, all matter is energy, and all energy vibrates at a specific frequency. These vibrations can be measured in hertz, a standard unit of frequency (or wave) of one cycle per second. Every rock, toad, table, and tree has its own vibration, solids vibrating slower than less dense matter like liquids and gas. The body vibrates not only as a whole but every molecule, cell, tissue, organ, gland, and bone in our body also has its own vibration. The HeartMath Institute has determined that the magnetic field of our heart generates the greatest field of any organ and reaches about ten feet beyond the physical body in all directions, which may explain how being in love is all-consuming, literally filling and overflowing our field.[10] Different emotions and brain states generate specific wave patterns, information that has contributed to the growing use of binaural beats as an audio therapy that relies on separate waves coming into the left and right ears to induce results like deepening sleep or heightening concentration.

Earth, too, vibrates and generates an electromagnetic wave pattern, referred to as the Schumann resonance. A series of extremely low frequencies in the Earth's electromagnetic field, these waves take place between its surface and the lower level of the ionosphere from the core at an average frequency of 7.83 Hz. Interestingly the Schumann resonance is the same brain wave frequency as that of an energy healer engaged with a client or a person in deep meditation, a correlation that led researchers to investigate the link between human health, consciousness, and the Earth's electromagnetic field.[11] A 2005 study found the Earth's field to impact blood pressure and possibly also heart rate and depression.[12]

The implications of studies like these are profound. Not only does everything vibrate and impact us, but those vibrations influence other vibrations. In her 2019 Bioneers keynote talk, environmentalist and writer Terry Tempest Williams referred to a scientific study confirming vibrations from the earth she has frequently felt. She says, "The earth has a pulse, as do we. No separation."[13] It gives new meaning to Jerry Lee Lewis's song lyrics referring to a "whole lotta' shakin' goin' on."

We live in an incredibly complex field of vibration. Everything is connected. Everything is alive. Subtle energy interacts with subtle energy, matter intermingles with matter, and the Earth body intimately connects with the human body, which connects to other bodies as linked living ecosystems. Referring to the symbiotic relationship between fungus and plants, forest ecologist Suzanne Simard acknowledges that "the chemicals that move through mycorrhizal networks are the same chemicals as neurotransmitters in our brain."[14]

What takes place in any one sector of this interconnected body or field influences what takes place in another, what philosopher Maurice Merleau-Ponty refers to as "intercorporeity" and what Buddhists call "interdependence." Touch the earth and by extension we are touching ourselves. Care for the Earth and we are caring for ourselves. The personal body is part of the larger body that is Earth. Matter, vibration, air, water, dirt, molecules, atoms, electromagnetic energy, and bioenergy intertwine with us. This mutual relationship has contributed to the establishment of new fields: ecosomatics, which connects embodiment practices with ecological practices, and ecopsychology, which similarly looks at the tie between human behavior and the natural world. Ecopsychologist Theodore Roszak sees the needs of our planet and ourselves as being on a continuum. Commenting about our abuse toward the land and our anthropocentrism, he says, "The epidemic psychosis of our time is the lie of believing we have no ethical obligation to our planetary home."[15] At fault is our willful blindness to anything that does not position the wants and immediate fulfillment of our ego as central. Many of us suffer a cultural amnesia that forgets the importance of our ancient ancestral home, the nutrients in the soil and elements and other trace particles in the atmosphere and biosphere, our global ecosystem that includes living organisms (biotic) and nonliving (abiotic) factors, all of which are vital to our continuation.

What ecosomatics and ecopsychology hold in common is recognizing the existence of relationships taking place constantly regardless of our awareness. By disregarding them, we fail to understand the ramifications of our role in the partnership with the larger picture. It's no surprise that relationship and connectivity can be challenging for Westerners adept at distinguishing our individuality. What sets us apart and above others is considered a hallmark of the culture. Thinking we are separate is a result of compartmentalized thinking, not a comprehensive or global truth. Says author Clarissa Pinkola Estés, "The body is like the earth . . . as vulnerable to overbuilding, being carved into parcels, cut off, overmined, and shorn of its power as any landscape."[16]

Devoting attention to relationship and connectivity leads to more consciously deepening an ecology of self that includes the larger biotic systems in which we partake. It's a reminder that we all participate in not only our own biological system, but every other biological, physical, psychological, social, ecological, and energetic system. Which is why every thought, feeling, and action matters. Every thought, feeling, and action vibrates. Every thought, feeling, and action creates its own chemical reaction. There are no isolated events. Everything connects. Every event big and small impacts other events if not in the same room or building, perhaps further afield, across town or the globe, our atoms, vibrations, and carbon emissions passing undetected through walls and national borders that separate us only to a degree.

Animals can detect a seismic tremor and approaching tsunami and will flee for safety before the ground visibly shakes and the sea overpowers the shore, their finely tuned senses able to sense early signs. Ants, regardless of their proximity to the colony, know if their queen has died and will cease work accordingly. Forester Peter Wohlleben, who recognizes that trees communicate and thrive when together, says, "the most astonishing thing about trees is how social they are. The trees in a forest care for each other, sometimes even going so far as to nourish the stump of a felled tree for centuries after it was cut down by feeding it sugars and other nutrients, and so keeping it alive."[17] Precognition and other psi phenomena may be explained by a similar heightened sensitivity; some of us are more sensitive to external factors than others, our sensory apparatus more finely tuned, our perceptual walls more permeable. Some of us listen within and find not only our inner world but also how it connects with the external world.

RESONANCE

Our field is a composite of vibrations that interacts with other fields fed by a multiplicity of subtle energies. Most of the time, we're too busy with the demands of the day to notice or we haven't been trained to sense them. What if that were to shift? What if we turned attention to the subtle phenomena of our body and perceived its contents? What if we extended awareness into the region surrounding our body, our field, what's sometimes referred to as negative space, and determine its apparent emptiness to be populated with all sorts of useful information? If you turn your attention here, some advice, especially for the uninitiated: Do so incrementally, lest you unnecessarily bombard and exhaust yourself with a torrent of impressions impeding any type of focus. Here's where grounding is essential. Opening perceptual gates can upend unresolved emotional and psychological issues and lead to confusing inner complexes with outer events. We may rattle unresolved anger and helplessness, the body spilling its stored memories and impressions too traumatic to process at the time. Additionally, the opening can excite the ego into believing the ability to detect expanded perceptions makes us special or extraordinary. Reality check: such abilities are accessible to any of us who take the time to familiarize ourselves with how these energies manifest. Better to wade in with a wise, discerning mind. Better to be alert to currents whose source and impact are not readily recognized. Be curious, yes, but go slowly.

Here's where embodiment and embodied cognition come into play: We root by necessity in our physical body, inhabiting ourselves by relying on the full array of our sensory abilities, feeling the experiences that are bodying self. Feel the placement of your feet upon the floor. Relax the jaw, shoulders, or any other part where tension is detected. Observe breath. Then take your awareness a step further and extend it to the energetic body and rely on your expanded senses to detect what shows up. Watch, witness, and wonder. Allow and question. Those initial instances of discovery can challenge who we are and what we thought was possible. Those instances can startle us into being more present to the peculiar and wondrous truths of our own experience. As the moment unfolds, it can transform the tenor of our being.

As if we're standing at the shore and seeing the ocean and distant horizon for the first time, there can be no turning back from such an exploration, no return to the limiting notion of self that believes itself separate from others, an island unto itself. Gaze broadens and awareness of the field liberates. The body softens, perceptions expand, and an integration of inner with outer and here with there takes place. As if encountering a long-awaited friend, as if inhaling into the sacrum and engaging the vagus nerve, as if discovering mystery and answer simultaneously, as if the effort of our actions retreats and reveals a moment that is lustrous and unfathomable. Awareness forever alters us, and we revise our definition of what is humanly possible.

I attribute resonance to my ability to see auric light, its first instance puzzling. As my eyes closed for bedtime sleep the evening prior to meeting a Tibetan teacher, I noticed a white spherical light move around my head. Initially I thought the light to be headlights from a car creeping down the road looking to park, except my glance out the window revealed no car, just the quiet dark of night. As soon as I lay back down and lowered my eyelids, the soft luminous sphere reappeared. A flashlight, I thought, as my eyes popped open, and I peered out the window looking for but not finding a neighbor or prowler.

When I met the teacher the following day, he asked what prompted me to request our meeting. Weeks earlier, I felt inexplicably compelled to meet in person, an unfamiliar sensation in my belly, a pull toward him that placed all other engagements on hold. But rather than say any of that, I told him it may have something to do with the light. He smiled, nodded, and invited me into his study. There we shared a long silence; conversation about perception, poetry, meditation, and movement; and then a wholly unfamiliar connection I hadn't known possible. My awareness roamed inside his body as if a spiritual or energetic drawbridge had lowered that allowed me to look around freely as it felt he was doing with me. Vibrations from his every word, breath, and slight motion penetrated me, a conduit between us open. The weight of my body lightened as if floating, awareness holding me in a strange, dreamlike place. "You were ready for a transmission," he said before I walked back to my car without adequate words to describe what had taken place, an initiation that shook me free, the commonplace having dropped its disguise, my usual filters gone.

Since then, most often while I meditate, dance, write, or give a healing session, various colored lights appear around my body or a client's. Each color emanates a specific feeling. For instance, white feels protective and gold feels numinous and otherworldly. Only a dark and murky color rouses my concern and suggests an energy block that is reluctant to release, a possible precursor to or signal of a serious illness. I use light, like the rise of emotion, to indicate a condition of the body and quality of consciousness, and sometimes summon it to activate a particular energy for balance or to strengthen health.

It's one thing to happen upon a resonant connection and quite another to seek it out intentionally. Being in conscious resonance with another ushers in an expanded sense of self and reveals us as composites of constantly changing conditions. Conscious resonance also leads to feeling complete, heightened sensitivity delivering community as close as our fingers. The resonance may be emotional, physical, intellectual, energetic, spiritual, or a combination, and opens channels of communication that establish synergy. This synergy does not homogenize or erase difference. Rather it supports the integrity of difference and lays down genuine paths to bridge differences. It relies on combining those differences to reach results larger than the sum of their parts. What is required is looking within, centering, and looking outward. The process establishes balance within, which simultaneously reinforces establishing balance with another. The process supports synching up, responsive to obvious and subtle bodily cues, and an awareness of breath intermingling with energy.

Synching up opens doors to the unknown, creates a fluid exchange, and establishes a transpersonal, sometimes transcendent connection. Just here. Just this. It may be my hand or yours, sound rising up from the throat or the gradual release of back tension. It can take place with a friend, a pet, a plant, water, and likely various objects. A young autistic acquaintance of mine had a pet metal pipe that he fondly carried with him in a pocket or in his hand. He explained it gave him comfort. When he held on to it, he stood straighter, and his feet did not supinate, which previously had threatened his balance. Only when he could stand and walk without losing his balance consistently did he finally abandon the pipe.

Resonance points toward something larger than individual consciousness, larger than a mind encased by a brain and skull, how consciousness is typically understood. When experienced from our usual perspective, we likely see it as an energetic extension of ourselves with parts that can move around like game pieces on a board. Extend that awareness further and attention gets liberated from our relative self. We enter an energy field that is centerless and infinite, no inner and outer, just a continuous field of presence, our awareness a concentration, one point among uncountable others, a me with a we.

Typically our words and gestures, as much as they connect us to others, paradoxically wall us in and keep another away. It's akin to the beverage held in front of our torso at a party that puts us at ease while chatting, the drink both helping in upholding a safe distance and permitting us to converse comfortably. Obviously words and gestures are an essential part of communicating, but another depth of exchange takes place when eyes meet without the smoke screen of words. The simple act of looking reveals the fleeting thoughts and emotions taking place without naming or analyzing any. We get to be present to the unnamed and preconceptualized somatic events as they take place and allow another to witness the wordless activity. These somatic events have been there all along, but what's different is the focus of attention, our usual defenses and deflections temporarily suspended. In its place is a vulnerable, intimate, visceral, and energetic connection, an empathic resonance, two bodies in the process of being and becoming, two bodies witnessing life unfold breath by breath.

Try This

Sit across from a friend or trusted family member and gaze into each other's eyes. Refrain from speaking. Look for a set time, perhaps ten minutes. Look while being looked at. Notice your thoughts, sensations, and feeling, and any shifts taking place. Notice what you're noticing.

When I've led somatic connecting exercises in workshops, participants regularly report feeling closer to their partner despite not sharing any details in words about their lives. When the exercise includes verbally reporting on what is noticed, one speaking while the other listens without commenting, what I refer to as somatic presencing, it alters the consciousness of both participants. The power of somatic presencing is tied to the impromptu sharing while a neutral witness listens without interruption, akin to unconditional acceptance, an exchange that heightens awareness of perceptions and is free of judgments.

Recent decades have advanced personal subjective embodiment through numerous practices like yoga, meditation, breath work, dance, and more. With the deep listening that is part of these practices, they reinforce coming home to the body and embodying ourselves with greater acceptance. Getting to know our thoughts, sensations, feelings, and energy connects us to the motion, expression, and continual shifts of our personal idiosyncratic body. These practices lead to increased intuition and embodied wisdom, a homing in that supports learning, growing, and integrating, all essential enlivening processes. They lead toward recognizing the patterns that hold us in place and deciding upon alterations that accord with our best intentions.

We're not done exploring and practicing personal embodiment. Far from it. Most of us are in the early stages of awakening to and fulfilling our potential, heightening awareness, and expanding consciousness. Too many of us continue to entertain unhelpful judgments along with individual and collective blind spots, all of which signal a need to enhance awareness. Too many filters remain carelessly and unconsciously in place. Too many circumstances trigger a falling out with ourselves. The path of clarity, self-compassion, wisdom, and wholeness requires regular vigilance to flesh out what is overlooked, dismissed, or negated. An embodiment practice can resolve any quarrels with ourselves, offer sensory input, provide insights, and establish a grace with a more inclusive reality of What Is. What Is awaits our attention. What Is awaits our sensitivity. What Is awaits our commitment, appreciation, curiosity, and awe. What Is warrants facing the positives and negatives of our life, the instances of fulfilling and falling short of our potential, knowing when our mind and heart open and when they close, what sensations and perceptions get discounted and which ones get elevated. All of it. We witness and practice being present to the entirety of our being with the compassion of a loving friend or family member. We witness our patterns without judgments to see their role in shaping our actions, thoughts, moods, work, and relationships, essentially our life. With greater awareness comes choice.

WE SPACE

Lagging behind in the development of personal embodiment is awareness of our shared personal spaces, our collective embodiment. I don't mean you and I sharing a table or sitting in the same restaurant but how ideas originating outside us show up within our skin, how policies we had no hand in creating impact our behaviors, how the language at our disposal influences what we perceive, and how another's mood influences our own.

Nascent in our development are interpersonal practices that contribute to coming to know what lives in our shared personal spaces. Not like yoga, which typically focuses on an individual body, but practices that are interconnected, intercorporeal, interrelational, transpersonal, and intersubjective. Consider a practice that feels into and is responsive to the field shared between people. Such practices are an unexplored and undeveloped frontier. Here the construct of I is recognized as We, not only a coupling of I's but the seemingly empty space between us. It's a matter of lifting our gaze and perspective from me and mine to us and ours, from my breath to our air, from my body and energy to a collective body and energy itself, from my house to a neighborhood, city, state, country, continent, or however far out into the cosmos we can go. We experience individual breath and sensation, track the arrival of thoughts and feelings, and then shift attention to what dwells beyond our dermal edge. It's a recognition that our senses extend farther than our common reach. It's a recognition that much resides between us. We notice what shows up. We come to know the kinesphere, the area that is an arm's length out from the body, and when ready, shift the focus farther out—or perhaps my language and direction are off, and reaching inward but with a more highly refined interoception. Either way, the organs of perception upgrade from 2.0 to 3.0 and lead to new information and abilities. Once the new operating system is engaged, we notice what shows up, contents that may be dreamlike or appear with startling clarity.

Here's where expanded perceptions come into play. Here's where we build upon the muscles of the five senses and rely upon input from the inner senses. Look for a faint sensation, an inkling of a thought, the flash of an image, an intuitive punch, the imagination yawning awake or working overtime. Information may come in on any sensory channel. Watch for what shows up on the screen of your attention. Regard as equal the dismissed and embraced information until you're able to discern the difference between fantasy and actual perception. The doors of perception open for those willing to jiggle the knob open. It's a matter of suspending common filters and broadening attention, of following breath and subtle energy, of making the effort and releasing control, of following hunches and glimmers with curiosity, of feeling okay about being unsettled and challenged, returning always to the ground of the present moment.

At a conference, I participated in an exercise in which we paired up with a stranger and were instructed to share information about the other without having first engaged in a conversation to find out any facts. Refer to a memory, a preoccupation, a concern, or whatever comes to mind. Don't think. Guess, if necessary. Approaching it as a light-hearted game, immediately images flashed into my awareness, leading me to tell my partner about his preferred vacation spot, the lounge chair that needed repair, his avoidance with his father, his preference for Italian food, the mozzarella dripping with olive oil, and how he might want to go ahead and apologize to his high school sweetheart. When the time was up, my partner asked how I knew these things about him. I didn't. Honestly it felt like I was making them up and had tapped into a stream of consciousness.

How could I have known those things? Perhaps an equally worthy question is how I could have not known. What cultural ideology or practice gets in the way of believing in the possibility of receiving such information? Cultural conditioning explains the reason why the Warlpiri people of Australia always know cardinal points, even in a windowless room.[18] Field dependence, a cognitive style defined by psychologist Herman Witkin, explains why one culture sees objects in the foreground and another primarily sees what's in the background.[19] Cultural conditioning could also explain doubting my ability to know information about a stranger without an exchange of words.

LIFE TASK

As we edge toward a new paradigm that includes more of our potential, shining a light into the unapparent or hidden areas of our being and interbeing may be among our most important life tasks and contribute to the solutions to our current challenges. In the twilight of consciousness lie the disowned parts of us awaiting attention, possibly our greatest hope toward wholeness and a habitable planet. It is the fertile region for growth, an area in need of attention, compassion, and curiosity, ultimately a space for personal and collective transformation. In its dim light healing takes place. In its shadow new life and abilities emerge. It is not a question of whether or not to engage in a practice that illuminates these areas, but rather when and how often. My response: Do so now. Do so with this moment, this word, this sorrow, this ache, this reflection, this wonder, this joy, this despair, this anomaly, this impulse, this breath, this glimpse. Be present to all levels of being to see what shows up. Pause the usual routine. Sit back or sit up. Take a look around and within. Reach out to a stranger if your tendency is to withdraw or be quiet if your tendency is to socialize. Walk among trees. Mix up habits. Rearrange the order of your day and how you go about activities. Employ underutilized intelligences. Move the enchanted place that is your body. Use imagination and intuition as guides for providing clues from the unconscious and from the usually obscured or ignored field. Note the small yet constant revisions of your body, each moment unfolding its subtle and obvious cues, its lights, form, and love. Locate the crumbs to find your way home.

It takes a commitment of time and attention devoted to a practice. It may be as simple as expressing a gratitude nightly before falling asleep or checking the breath several times throughout the day, practices that increase ease. With any practice done often enough, the benefits build and spill into multiple areas of our life. The focus and stillness from my years of sitting on a meditation cushion do not end once I put on my shoes and head out the door. The effects stay with me in encounters with colleagues, cashiers, and distracted drivers. They stay with me when I walk with a student in the hall or carry the trash to the bin in the alley. Stumbles and distractions are inevitable, but it's a matter of identifying them and finding the way back to balance and the welcome home of my body.

A regular practice reveals insights that arrive slowly and intermittently, a confiding that arrives like a reliable friend whose support and advice we may take for granted periodically. A regular practice is akin to tending a garden that requires tilling, watering, and fertilizing, possibly years before flowering and fruiting. Its insights show up incrementally, which we're more likely to recognize if keeping a journal to document change. Insights may also burst through the ordinary commotion of our attention like a cork's sudden release from its bottle. These insights, or peak experiences, break us open. They may provoke a stumble and ache. They may disrupt our thoughts and belief systems and temporarily throw us off balance. They leave us having to decide how or if to use them. They may be the catalyst toward growth (preferably) or prompt us to clutch the status quo of the familiar.

It's great to experience a peak experience or aha moment when the busyness and confusion of life erupts into making sense, when the noise of the day quiets, when our heartache with the ills of the world finds a salve, when we touch into the miracle of breath, body, mind, energy, and spirit working together, when an evolutionary impulse compels an expansion of consciousness. The relief that accompanies such experiences is incomparable. There is no deeper sigh, no further longing. Just the nervous system settled, the body stirred by rest and awake to its dream. Our highest ambition, to body our authentic self, is realized, and in that moment, there's nothing we need to do, no other vocation worth pursuing, no other want left unsatisfied.

Years ago during one of my college dance classes, my teacher pressed me to extend my limbs further and not hold back. "More," she yelled from across the room. "Further!" Shyness and years of asthma inhibited my movements, yet I pushed beyond my usual limits. My legs lifted higher, arms and fingers reaching outward as I crossed the room repeatedly, my heart pounding. Suddenly my breath halted and something in my chest twinged. Then the pain that typically accompanied my physical exertions disappeared altogether as breath filled my torso unimpeded and flooded me with energy. Not only did I perform the requested movements without pain, but I did so effortlessly as if tasked with something as easy as tapping a finger. When class ended, I slipped into my street clothes, then sprinted across campus to my next class with uncharacteristic vigor. Breath replaced lethargy with vibrancy and a realization about its profound importance. Yes, breathing is autonomic, but when done with a degree of control as is the case with practices like yogic pranayama, it opens the body to new abilities. The breakthrough led to exploring my breath further and overcoming the limits brought about from asthma.

A challenge of a peak experience is a tendency to want to stay put, even as circumstances change. Who in their right mind wants to leave paradise? Yet staying is impossible because we and the place continually shift, small and big changes inevitable, impermanence a reminder to let go and practice balancing through grounding and adjusting. If we have the luxury of reflection or the necessity of change, what it calls for is finding a way to integrate the new experience.

Hannah came to me after undergoing radiation for cancer and leaving an abusive husband. Her body was tender and overly sensitive to touch. Ungrounded, she tiptoed around the room and spoke rapidly. Her field was collapsed from her pelvis down to her feet. Her peak moment came as a realization that she deserved to be happy and healthy, which coincided with a rush of sensation and trembling throughout her body. By the next session, however, she doubted the insight. Hannah was so used to her husband's verbal and emotional abuse that it was difficult for her to recognize and believe in her strengths. By grounding her energy again and teaching her to stand and walk with the heels and balls of her feet, she was able to accept and integrate the recent insight.

We may experience a peak moment as so unsettling and disruptive, a threat to our belief system and understanding of the world, that we push the experience away, ignore or repress it. In a culture focused on outward achievements, not inward reflection, emotional growth, energetic shifts, or spiritual development, we may feel confusion, shame, or horror, ill-equipped to understand the gift bestowed upon us. It may take time or a good teacher to show us how the emotional or mystical state that accompanies our peak experience is a welcome invitation to grow and move beyond our usual filters and constructs.

Holding aha moments lightly, sitting in awe as we might do with a sudden rain shower in a cloudless sky, slows the habit of conceptualizing and translating the experience into the ideas and language of our subscribed paradigm, which can diminish the impact of the breakthrough. Rushing to understand the breakthrough may quash its momentum and reduce the extraordinary to ordinary, the glow to a flicker, awe to insouciance. A more advisable approach is to be engaged as actor and audience, driver and passenger, the roles blurred, difference undifferentiated. It may prompt a fit of laughter or a bout of crying. It may provoke a need to take off from work and go backpacking. It may bathe us in an unfamiliar magic as we witness the wondrous way life unfolds. Maintain equilibrium in this between state, not quite here or there, or here and everywhere else simultaneously, a GPS nightmare but also a paradise, the compass pointing where it is and needs to be.

Holding these moments lightly enables us to ride their waves with minimal interference from the constraints, diminishments, or aggrandizements of ego. William James knows these regions well and refers to them as "states of insight into depths of truth unplumbed by the discursive intellect. They are illuminations, revelations, full of significance and importance, all inarticulate though they remain; and as a rule they carry with them a curious sense of authority."[20] Better to witness what longs to be, the I Amness of an ever-present, ever-changing awareness, being on the cusp of becoming. Ungraspable and elusive, the territory of artists, poets, and mystics, it is the formless playing with form, life emerging and receding and emerging endlessly, the body animating breath, contradictions and paradox everywhere as pervasive as spring pollen. Those in the know realize they don't know.

If choosing to explain such experiences, it may be inevitable that we translate it according to our stage of development, into our available language and understanding, into the safety of the previously known. Admittedly, it's hard to frame it in expansive language full of the awe of the unfolding mystery, to say this but also that, a tension of opposites that becomes revelatory. Hopefully we have enough awareness to avoid dogmatism, zealotry, and spiritual bypassing.

Whether the insight takes place slowly over many years as a result of an ongoing practice or is a sudden rupture arriving out of nowhere, its cause equally mystifying, it's helpful to find a way to integrate into our understanding. I do not believe there is one foolproof method to do so. Question, trust, allow, read, reflect, join a like-minded group, or find a mentor. Use it to inspire and inquire. Use it as a watering can to grow understanding and abilities. Use it to send breath from the lungs into the pelvis.

Summer months in my backyard bring the arrival of fireflies emitting their bioluminescence to attract mates and ward off predators. Many a dusk I sit outside to watch the light show, the flashes igniting my amazement at witnessing nature's beauty. I imagine a collective peak event to look similarly, a cascade of embodied awakening, a recognition of familial connection linked by DNA and atoms, solo dances performed simultaneously by a troupe, an unmistakable tide of awareness invigorating nature, a rededication of purpose, a revisioning of the body that includes healing, maturing, and energetic embodiment. We nurture what we love. We turn inward and find another. We turn toward another and find ourselves.

5

The Embodiment of Expanded Perceptions

The living body is always going beyond what evolution, culture and language have already built.

EUGENE GENDLIN

A few days into a silent Zen retreat, I was tasked with serving cookies. Had I been at home, the job would have involved me casually dumping them onto a plate and placing them on a table central to my guests. There is nothing casual about a Zen meditation retreat wherein activities are designed to still and awaken the mind to its habits.

In the kitchen away from fellow retreatants, as instructed, I placed each cookie top side up an inch apart from the next one to create a grid on a tray. Then I carried the tray to the meditation room to walk a designated route to serve the teacher first, everyone else after. I stood between two people whose hands were folded on their laps, their gaze downward. When I lowered myself to a kneel, the awaiting meditators brought palms together to acknowledge my presence before taking a cookie. There is no chitchat; no eye contact, either. My focus remains on the tray and the hand that comes into the frame of my vision to retrieve a cookie. Once the people on either side of me take one, I rise and repeat the exercise with those farther down the line until the entire room is served.

Nothing like days without talking and ample sitting upon a cushion facing a wall to shift awareness and render the cookie taking as telling a gesture as any psychological test. The hand of my first taker glided above the tray before landing efficiently on the selection as if following through on a flight plan. Others were not as deliberate. Some hands hovered hesitantly over several cookies as if choosing the right one was as momentous as deciding upon a new job. Some plucked the cookie with all fingers, others with thumb and index fingers, another with the tips of the thumb and pinky. As if adhering to a cosmic baking rule, a few chose based on the grid, selecting or ignoring the cookie at the corner of the tray, in the center, or the one closest by.

This brief inconsequential activity distinguished one taker's mood, thought process, and personality from the next person's and rendered an entire exchange nonverbally. I was astounded by how much it revealed, my haptic sense and ability to read body language not previously applied to details of desert selection. The exchange made clear how much we rely on verbal language for communication, which we do to great effect, but also to our detriment.

Words are everywhere—on clothing tags, food packages, electronics manuals, bills, traffic signs, train tickets, even on the body in the form of tattoos. In a text-based culture, verbal literacy is considered a sign of intelligence and a handicap for those who can't read. Certainly the necessity and precision of words is beneficial as seen in the difference between *weather* and *thunderstorm* and *love* and *lust.* They're useful in providing specific instruction, such as the difference between meeting "at the airport" versus meeting "on the lower-level baggage claim, door C," the former of which may have us circling the terminals until a follow-up text with more specific details.

Categories, specificity, and nuances in meaning enable discourse on complex topics in need of braiding or untangling. We use language for speculation, imagination, vision, debate, explication, planning, and conclusion. We use it to create a comprehensive order from what was previously senseless and amorphous. Writers unify world with word by engaging language's rhythms, imagery, syntax, sound, definitions, and structure to make a point and provide a verbal experience. Of course writing is not the only communicative medium available, but language carries a particular potency, especially at times of need, when the world seems at odds with us, when our ability to cope lags behind our vulnerability and we need an expressive outlet. Relying on writing for expression and the organization of ideas, novelist Toni Morrison says, "This is precisely the time when artists go to work. . . . We speak, we write, we do language. That is how civilizations heal."[1]

Words are a dynamic system interfacing with time and histories that are ours and sometimes only tangentially ours by chance of birth or adopted country. Writing and speaking create a pattern from this system, transforming nebulous impressions into a narrative and meaning. It's how we understand ourselves and culture and how we cultivate, welcome, or resist change. It's why we write. It's why, too, we read, to lose ourselves to the landscape of another's mind and to find ourselves.

Concepts and specific words influenced our perceptions and beliefs. They function as sound, meaning, emotion, vibration, a pattern of energy leading us one way or another. We may not recognize a phenomenon without a word pointing it out. Consider *quantum entanglement* or *mansplaining*. Propagandists manipulate language to their benefit. Consider how *fake news* got many to question truth and spread misinformation. Words set off a chain reaction of impressions. They cast spells. They get us to think or envision what might not otherwise have entered our mind.

Writing is an important enough activity that I devote hours and months to it year after year. Always it guarantees at least one reader: oneself. This singular reader is important in enabling expression, reflection, and drawing connections between ideas. We pause long enough from other activities to listen within and exercise sensing tied to verbal expression. Writing acts as smoke signals sent to ourselves. It encapsulates a process, the trail of a story, a poem, a narrative weaving loose threads into a perceptible pattern, the formless provided form. It is breath made visible and intelligible enough to allow us to read ourselves. The power of the page affords us a malleable space for being.

The power of writing lures me back repeatedly with its siren of beauty that delivers me safely to its shore. To an extent, I don't fully know who I am or what I think and feel until I listen to the moment, the verbal flow ensues, and I later read what's written. Even then, the lines spill multiple connotations and require multiple rereads, the focus at any given moment eclipsing a more complete understanding. Filters operate continually. Think you have a handle on the truth? You do, but there are always overlooked and missing parts.

DIRECT EXPERIENCE

Words shine their light and shadow everywhere and, among their many uses, are particularly potent in helping us think. Therein, also, lie their limitations. Words give the impression of solidifying concepts and beliefs. A noun such as *mouse* or *freedom* suggests a staid definition unless we consult a dictionary or approach language with a poet's or philosopher's eye. If allowed, words can get in the way of actual perceiving. They can eclipse other views and obstruct direct experience.

With direct experience, we set aside concepts, beliefs, habits, and cultural conditioning. We set aside the known in favor of sensing. We feel into What Is. Attention redirects to any of the five senses and to the inner senses. Look with the eyes but perhaps also the inner eyes. Feel with fingertips and skin but also extend the haptic sense to subtle energetic tendrils. Shift focus to what is immediate and shows up on the screen of your attention: the empty glass on the table, the light reflecting, awareness of shoulder tension, of inhaling deeply, of licking lips, of a vague something near the left side of the head, an inexplicable warmth. Become intimate with What Is even if it's unfamiliar and hard to recognize, even if it stumps a predilection for quickly identifying and rushed conceptualizing.

Direct experience clears away mental, emotional, and energetic clutter. Bodily tensions relax and give way to a spaciousness that is startlingly real. Colors appear more saturated; lines demarcating shape contain both greater contrast and less. All impressions spill into everything else, the dualism that shaped perceptions yielding to something more complex, dynamic, and pure. A pen is a pen but is also a compass needle pointing to a direction of thought and perspective. A family member leaves the room, but their energetic signature lingers behind. Last night's dream is a template of today. The light of the mind tied to the sensing body illuminates its shadows. Everything reflects. We close our eyes to energy pulsing.

Direct experience can be disorienting and unnerving. All is not what it was or what we believe it should be. The frame and contents have shifted. It's like the sudden loss of electricity; the hum of the appliances quiet, the display on the digital clock disappears, and the room darkens. No more computer work, no recharging the phone, and no hot dinner. We leave the room to retrieve a flashlight and candles, yet habitually flick the light switch in the closet despite the futility. Our usual trajectory of activities abruptly halted, we sit in the dark unsure of what to do and impatient for power to be restored.

It's that pause that is of great interest and frequently contains unimagined opportunity. When the conditioned mind turns off, when expectations fall aside, when the default of our habits stop, when thinking's fallibility is revealed, our senses rise to the occasion, and we get to practice somatic literacy. We feel the surroundings imposed upon us with heightened awareness. Our hand grazes the wall as we walk the darkened hallway, and we poke our fingers into the closet drawer to fumble for the candles and flashlight. We hear our heart beating and feel a nervous excitement while negotiating the new landscape. Our senses intensified, we touch what is present. Oddly, the present seems to have more texture, volume, or scent, a flicker or flash where before there was nothing—or so we thought.

No ideas, only sense. Listen and feel. Look around and within. Anchor awareness in the body. Watch how you perceive phenomena. Watch how you trust or doubt the senses. Watch how you interpret and misinterpret events.

By anchoring in the body—embodying—focus shifts to the inflow and outflow of energy, to breath, to patterns dissolving and reforming, emotion, sensation and energy in motion, ripples and flux everywhere. Blocked or narrowed attention opens. Both brain hemispheres are engaged. New sights, perceptions, intuitions, and neural pathways form.

Just this moment.

This silence or cacophony.

This sensation. That one, too.

This return to the body.

"I'm seeing colors," says my client, Phil. "Purple around my head, blue at my throat. What's going on? What does it mean?"

"We'll discuss it in a bit," I reply. "For now, simply be a witness. Be present with your body without thinking. Notice feelings and sensation. Do as little as possible."

I, as much as Phil and other clients who have plied me with questions about their strange perceptions while on the massage table, want to know what's going on. Unfamiliar events and perceptions take place regularly on the table. Off the table, too, as several of the stories in this book show.

So what *is* going on? What is this body, and what is it capable of?

How these questions are answered is determined by who does the answering and the filters they uphold. For instance, a classical physicist may define the body as a combination of oxygen, carbon, hydrogen, nitrogen, calcium, and phosphorus. A medical doctor likely experiences the body anatomically as a collection of tissues, organs, and systems. A religious person likely understands the body as matter, soul, and spirit. And an energy healer is likely to include subtle matter and vibration. I say yes to all of these. The body is not any one thing, its shape, size, content, and definition dependent on age, circumstances, culture, and attention, all undergoing constant change. In any given moment, the body is more able or less, more free or less, somewhere on the continuum of conscious and oblivious of itself.

As an energy medicine practitioner, somaticist, poet, dancer, and meditator with an open, sensitive, and inquisitive nature, I access multiple perceptual channels through touch, motion, words, energy, and silence, the particulars of one enhancing and redefining another. Each is a language that lights up different parts of the brain assisting in the perception of phenomena. Playing in the field of any one of them, or with a combination of them, can lead to experiencing uncommon levels of consciousness. This type of consciousness, chiseled or blurry, expansive or focused, is extraordinary and outlandish. Notably, it's also unremarkable and banal in that it's always right here as common as air, but it requires switching the channels of perception to perceive.

How far is the reach of consciousness? It depends on the method of travel and finesse of our senses. It depends on how we self-limit. It depends on what we believe. It depends on how we live in the home of our body connected to the body of Earth.

Within reach is interoception, an awareness of sensations within the body, from its organ systems, from cellular respiration, from the flesh and energy of being. This internal perceiving supports identifying, accessing, and appraising internal bodily signals, a process none too easy because awareness is not a given but must be developed as it draws from material that lives along the continuum of consciousness and unconsciousness. Harvard Business School professor Gerald Zaltman goes so far as to claim that 95 percent of our thinking is unconscious.[2] All the more reason to write, draw, dance, listen, and meditate, to lift the unconscious to the surface, to bring the hidden into view, to voice the silence. Says fiction writer Clarice Lispector about writing, "The world has no visible order and all I have is the order of my breath. I let myself happen."[3]

When we let ourselves happen, the body is allowed its breath and breadth. Energetic, emotional, and mental patterns relax and create a spaciousness. Patterns established in childhood and from trauma, loss, habits, and conditioning—all of which impact us and form our body—shift. The mind opens to what was previously off-limits. Sadness, despair or any other default emotion toggles toward joy, curiosity, anger, or whatever else naturally arises. Feelings previously locked away are released. The body in flow is allowed its grow. What was foreground recedes into the background or the backdrop gains new details. The story that was our life revises. Healing deemed impossible becomes possible. We reestablish a relationship with the personal self, which we find is connected to all else. To be in touch with the body means being in touch with influences, a relationship of mutuality, of give and take, of gravity holding us in place even as we move of our own volition.

We enter the dream and reality of our lives. Awareness continuously blinks. We sense this, which may be familiar or unfamiliar, then something else. We consider what wants to emerge, sensing along the way, guided by the body's intelligences without rushing headstrong to conclusions that may be ill-fitting or antiquated. We balance at the edge of sensing and understanding, one touch or glimpse or sound or footstep after another, all the while remaining intimate with our flesh and its field of energy moment by moment instantiating, our process of attention and allowing determining what manifests and what continues to hibernate.

The repercussions of this embodied homecoming, both calming and invigorating, locates us within our body and situated in place. We discover how we are part of, not apart from, the environment and Earth itself. By coming home to the body, dancer and philosopher Sondra Fraleigh says not only "body comes to mind," but mind comes to body and "the earth of the body and its natural intelligence, is tilled."[4] Embodying shows Earth reaching into and touching us, as us, as simultaneously we stand and feed upon Earth, the minerals of our body the same as those around us.

Try This

You can do this either standing or seated. Place your feet firmly on the floor. Imagine that a window at the arches of the feet opens. What comes in is earthly energy, the planet's vibration, its breath. Exiting the window is an exhalation of energy no longer personally needed. If it helps, imagine the exchange with color. Make any small adjustment like spreading toes or elongating the spine to amplify the process. Keep your awareness on the soles of your feet. Notice what you notice.

Frequently I do a version of this grounding exercise before facilitating a healing session to stay in flow and not take on a client's imbalance. Grounding exercises are foundational to practicing martial arts like t'ai chi or tae kwon do. This ability to somatically and energetically connect to Earth connects us to the felt sense of the present moment and our body's alignment. It also expands awareness to this radically changing planet that we need for survival. To be in dialogue with blood, breath, tissue, and bones, we are, by extension, in dialogue with air, dirt, water, fungus, plants, birds, and beasts. Grounding shares similarities with the Japanese practice of *shinrin-yoku,* or forest bathing—an ecotherapy where participants go to a forest or any natural habitat and immerse themselves in nature to lower anxiety and blood pressure and improve their health.[5]

SHOWING UP RESPONSIVELY

My intention in these pages has been to stir consciousness into a froth of awakening, for disjunctive experiences to lead to big and small ahas, to provoke somatic openings that expand perceptions and broaden awareness. For us to further who we are, aligned with the life force, the evolutionary pulse, to trust our senses and experience wholeness, to bring about a renaissance of our being. A lack of harmony and incoherence within us, the inner world extending to the outer world, contributes to societal discord. Too many of us are self-critical, withhold key parts of ourselves, and are growth averse. We accept too many of the dictates of society's biases that diminish the full range of our abilities, which makes us susceptible to internalized oppression, a wound cutting into our psychic well-being. We withdraw in fear, queasy, reactive, easily distracted from our higher purpose. Or we are lulled into a complacency with short-term rewards at the expense of long-term benefits.

There's no better moment than now to abandon denials and short-sightedness and stand (or sit or dance or walk) responsively in who we are. We are being called to investigate and nurture self, a deep respect tied to our flourishing. We are being called to recognize this moment in history with its sorrows, losses, fears, loves, and births as a growth edge. We are being called to rise up to the occasion to adjust ourselves accordingly. Step back or sideways, tilt the head or a belief, watch clouds or the parade of our thoughts. Situate ourselves firmly in the present open to the flow of being.

"Look out," yells the small voice who's been at our side all along but takes until now for us to hear. The voice or nudge or vision is meant to startle us awake, to adapt, shift, grow, and transform, to unveil who we are, to reorganize our sense of self tied to all else, to summon our potential into action, to recognize who we've been all along, but it has taken a crisis of our collective well-being to be revealed.

This awakening includes finding a healthy balance between being a passive recipient and active creator, being consciously and expansively present while participating in and trusting life's unfolding, recognizing the filters we entertain and tossing those that have expired. This is a process any of us can midwife alone or with the support of a select group or individual. This transformation toward wholeness is not only a revolution of individual consciousness, a catalyst for growth and expanded awareness, but also a revolution of cultural consciousness, the work of one influencing the many.

Such is the power of words.

Such is the power of stillness and silence.

Such is the power of a practice that places us on the front line emerging.

Such is the power of actions engaged in with integrity, authenticity, and awareness, an embrace of the totality of life as the impetus for change not merely for the sake of change—one disembodiment replacing another, one thoughtless reaction filling in for another, one dysfunction replacing another, one short-term solution acting as a temporary patch—but as an evolutionary shift. By stepping embodied into the fullness of who we are, what takes place is a transformation and a coherence of personal well-being that extends to all sentient and insentient beings and marks us as responsibly partaking in the ecology of self and the planet. What takes place is alignment with the present moment, which reaches out infinitely. Our focus: here, now, this. Fill in the blanks with your personal observations. Witness the surface and depth of being. Feel, look, and listen.

A tall order, I know. But I've seen what happens when we bring home exiled parts of us, when we apply patience and compassion to our unvoiced parts. Intrapersonal and interpersonal connections restore when we practice self-acceptance and embody ourselves more fully. The life current weakened by personal and societal wounding recharges and connections thought to be missing return. We sense and notice. We pay attention to the hints. We make connections. We enliven. We beneficially participate in the alchemy of the body. Nature nurtures us.

Jake attended my Writing from the Body class, which is devoted to writing, movement, and somatic awareness. In the first session, his despair was evident in his rounded shoulders, downcast gaze, a soft, uncertain voice, and a dark field. He wrote about taking up weight lifting in high school to combat getting bullied for his height and slight build. Though the bullying stopped, and he was now in college, he had little motivation to study, eat well, or get out of bed. A doctor prescribed antidepressants, yet their promised relief failed to manifest. "No one cares" he wrote in his journal, a justification for him to pick on others, perpetuating some of the very actions that harmed him originally. As I guided students to notice and respond to sensations and emotions, to stand in and embody their authentic self, his breath deepened, his spine elongated, his chest opened, and his shoulders unrounded. The shifts enabled him to feel his hurt without his usual armoring. He wrote in his journal about discovering new energy. He described his heart as "prickly" previously, but the exercise led to it "softening." He felt more alert. Soon after, his sought-after but elusive motivation returned, and he gained insight into his hurt-fueled reactivity. He shifted from being in dissonance and a hostage to his pain to being grounded in embodied awareness. He took up writing poems, which he eagerly shared with the class. His healing had begun in earnest.

Likely, every one of us has experienced a wound that impedes the flow of our vital energy. The pain may have taken place within the family or outside the home, the scars physical, emotional, spiritual, or some combination. Regardless of the severity of the wound, the result is the same; part of us withdraws and goes into hiding. The body contracts. We push the episode away, try to forget, perhaps deny it ever took place. A part of us disembodies, even dissociates (for those who suffered chronic pain or abuse), creating a rift between body and mind, feeling and knowing, refusing and accepting. We coped by creating a false self that helped us to adapt. The false self created defensive strategies for navigating the tricky terrain. Though this adaptive mechanism was helpful at the time, it becomes unhelpful when it overrides our authentic self and becomes the status quo long after the cause of our pain has passed. An unhealed wound can fester behind the scenes like a malevolent puppeteer sabotaging our aspirations, feelings, and thoughts, essentially how we inhabit our body.

Many of us leave the situation as is. We move on. What's done is done. Why make trouble for ourselves and stir up the past? The effort and pain involved in unearthing the memories is not worth our time. More pressing concerns like work and family occupy our attention.

WHOLENESS MATTERS

There's good reason to look. We stir up the past because the past is present. Because every event of our life is imprinted upon our flesh, in our cells, in muscle memory, in the visited and neglected areas of the body, and in the energetic field. We confront the pain to be in a generative flow of our life, not beholden to a past action, but to choose what works best for us now. We face the pain for healing to take place, which allows us to embrace and rightfully grow into our gifts.

Here's another compelling reason to look. We face the pain because our thoughts, actions, and feelings influence others directly and indirectly, which makes our personal healing collectively beneficial. Our healing contributes toward addressing the collective malaise and societal dysfunction toward well-being for the many. When we honor ourselves, we give another permission to do the same. When we bless who we are, our very nature, we are blessing nature itself.

A collective wound shows up in a similar way as an individual wound. There is contraction, resistance, denial, a twist on truth. But here it's a body of ideas and a group of people who clutch a sentiment or ideal whose usefulness and vitality have waned—or it wasn't helpful at the get-go. The wound may not be recognized as such because the number of people exhibiting the behavior normalizes the behavior or attitude. Consider the despondency of refugees who have spent years at a camp continuously thwarted from setting up a home and pursuing their aspirations and the apathetic staff that keeps them locked up.

Well-run businesses and organizations know that their survival depends on recognizing and adapting to change. Looking away, denying growth and the inevitability of changing circumstances can make an organization obsolete and hasten their demise. Kodak, once the leader in photography, got into the digital game too late and watched their profits spiral downward until they were forced to file for bankruptcy.

Healing is much more than the absence of pain. Rather, it indicates our degree of wholeness, a confluence of our physical, emotional, mental, spiritual, and energetic selves. In wholeness, there's no need to pretend or defend. Instead we operate from flow, from an experience of support and balance, from engaging in actions that enhance connection and embodiment and establish our body as home.

Osteopaths refer to the palpable *stillpoint,* a temporary cessation of the craniosacral rhythm of the spine, a profound rest that instigates healing and perception of wholeness. When a stillpoint is reached, it allows the body to enter a deep state of rest and recovery, which contributes to an increase in well-being and wholeness. We rest in the present moment, in breath, and in the flow of being.

Wholeness is another term for an integrated self. An integrated self makes room for thinking and feeling, for common and anomalous experiences, for inner and outer actions, for focused and expansive perceptions, for being that isn't egocentric, but ecocentric or even cosmocentric. An integrated self values the questions as much as the answers, acknowledges pain, finds ease in unease, and values curiosity, growth, compassion, love, and connection, knowing that life is rooted in these principles. An integrated self assists in establishing and developing our many intelligences, not only the ones promoted by our family and culture. An integrated self rides the turbulent and calm waves of circumstances, loosening and tightening the hold as necessary.

A term associated with wholeness is *coherence*. Researchers with the HeartMath Institute see coherence as a measure of the pattern in the heart's rhythm synchronized with various systems in the body such as the heart, respiratory system, and blood-pressure rhythms. They discovered the importance of synchronizing the powerful energy waves of the heart with those of the brain to encourage optimal well-being. Those experiencing coherence "reported increased creativity, enhanced communication with others, and a richer experience with the emotional textures of life . . . their perception of problems or difficult situations often widened enough that new perspectives and solutions emerged."[6] Notably they also recognized the strength of one person's heart waves positively impacts others.

Biologist Carla Hannaford echoes similar ideas. She says, "By maintaining our coherence, we can consciously retrain our senses to be more available to the rich vibrational fields around and within us, giving us full access to learning, intuition, and high-level reasoning."[7]

Contributing to coherence is engaging in a creative practice because it makes room for the unconscious to come out from hiding. The unconscious material need not be understood or analyzed. In fact, it may be best to leave it raw initially while the inspiration is fresh, sweeping up what's in its path, the censor and critic relieved from their usual obligation. The unfettered mind engaged in creative expression unhitches from the restraints of the ego to embrace bursts, fragments, and flows of information, impressions, rhythms, and nuance. We engage the medium with curiosity and regard expression as a sacred, life-sustaining act.

Like any heightened moment, we ride on the creative currents and keep our mind and ego from impeding the flow. We yield control to its pulse. The flux of the universe, the culture, and the body as process is provided a stage, easel, and voice. What wants to emerge or has been hesitant is given a chance to show, be it ambiguous, colorful, strident, symbolic, or whatever else. The imagination can run or sketch, tinker, or dream. Consider it a laboratory for being, our primordial wonder allowed to wander, abilities improving from the stretch, the executive areas of the brain relaxing while other areas perk up to establish new synaptic connections. We rebody and renew.

When ready, we can look closer to analyze, revise, add another layer of color, clarify an ambiguity, reflect upon the throbs of unconscious material, learn what has shifted, and unfold meaning. We contemplate and investigate. We sit back and move forward. The unknown becomes known, the interior experience becomes exterior, and the sanctuary of being and becoming is graced by our attentiveness and lights up the space of our wholeness.

The shift of one influences the many. The actions and thoughts of one influence the many. Our waking up stirs another. Our opening and healing stir another. Our authenticity and steps toward wholeness inspire another. Waves, vibrations, and influence everywhere.

Try This

Set a timer for twenty minutes and write every word, thought, and impression that comes to mind. Refrain from thinking. Keep the writing going without concern for making logical sense. Record words, phrases, and fragments, letting each one roll into the next. Do this same activity over consecutive days for maximum benefit.

Experiencing wholeness gets us into flow. Flow gets us to experience the give with the take, one action spilling into another, a coherence between our abilities and external conditions. Effort balances with effortlessness. The inner critic works in tandem with support. Obstacles that appear are regarded as characteristics, par for the course, not insurmountable impediments. We adapt. We ride the tumultuous and smooth waves of being. The senses sharpen and settle. We feel at liberty to expand into new territory, to experience the pliancy of skin, the permeable boundaries between ourselves and another.

Within reach always is our breath. Welcoming it into our body is a generative act. Welcoming it into the connective tissue often sealed off by tension brings about vitalizing ease.

From a place of wholeness and coherence, all actions, thoughts, and feelings are valuable as information, steps in a process, a detail of a larger picture. Interconnection appears everywhere, between the sound of my voice and its energy, between physics and algebra, history and philosophy, creativity and logic. Between bees and tomatoes, a snarl and a smirk, our breath and a neighbor's, those a brief walk away and those on the other side of the globe. We see the Kali and Phoenix principles at work, how suffering gives rise to despair, despair gives rise to pause, pause gives rise to insight, and insight gives rise to action. Not that this is a call for breakdown and suffering. But it is a call to use a breakdown, wound, or illness as a sign alerting us to some part being out of sync and to use it as an opportunity to reevaluate, reconsider, and transform. It's a call to celebrate what's been overlooked and to grow. It's a call to heal individually and collectively. It's a call to check in and remember all of who we are and dwell as a body in an ongoing vitalizing process.

Let me give you a peek behind the curtain of this page at a way I check in. Several sentences ago, I got out of the chair, turned up the music, and danced near the bookshelf and couch, away from the stacks of papers and tangle of electrical cords. My writing maintains a flow by periodically taking a break from verbalizing to stretch, twist, and bend. The rhythm of movement syncs me up with experiencing sensation and embodiment, breath deepening, stretches reinvigorating, the recently written echoing within and pulling me toward consequent expression. Interspersing dancing with writing reinforces flow and wholeness.

Breathe, write, move, flow, look, and listen in no specific order. One enhancing another shows a resonance between words and movement and recharges my battery.

Coming from a place of wholeness encourages releasing any limiting beliefs and fear-based reactions or whatever else gets in the way. The fallout from the decision to embrace wholeness, to be in touch, is to align with our authentic self. It's a choice. We choose to show up to who we are, heart and mind opening, body continually making small adjustments, perceptions expanding. We· become available. We open. We retire useless habits and adopt ones that are more effective. We let rise a deepening of sensing and realizing, there all along, but only now acknowledged, our perspective broadening to include this additional perspective. The choice leads to previously unseen possibilities and positions us in a profound, embodied knowing responsive to life's unfolding. We are positioned at a growth edge that is a leading edge, each breath carrying in restorative air and nutrients, each breath positioning us in the moment ripe with possibilities.

My recent movement activity refreshed me. Whatever mental and energetic cobwebs that formed as I sat with my computer are gone. I feel my belly while writing. I feel my back and jaw. Worn synaptic pathways are relieved by the redirection. The flow of writing resumes. Being unfolds in the verbal stream.

Try This

Notice the position of your body as you read this line. Move to make yourself more comfortable. Adjust your spine. Put both feet on the floor. Relax your shoulders and jaw. Take a deep breath. Look around the room before you return your gaze to the page. What details in your looking grab your attention? Where do those details lead to in yourself? What shows up that you hadn't noticed previously?

A decision to embrace wholeness has profound, far-reaching repercussions, impacting the energetic field and contributing to a wave of change. Every one of our actions matter by influencing the field. Journalist Malcolm Gladwell refers to the tipping point as the moment when an idea, trend, or social behavior crosses a threshold and spreads.[8] Researchers at Rensselaer Polytechnic Institute have found that when 10 percent of the population holds an unshakable belief, it gets adopted by a majority of people.[9] Spiritual teachers speak of transmissions, the sharing of evocative information through meditation, physical gestures, and words, some of us more keen at emitting and receiving than others. Consider deliberately sharing restorative and uplifting acts of kindness, concern, and love, each one part of the pulsing life force.

Wholeness and coherence align us not only with ourselves and others but with gravitational forces, the waves of Earth and the cosmos, the penultimate expanded field. A personal field is recognized as part of a much larger field. Groups like the Global Coherence Initiative formed to test and facilitate a shift in global consciousness from instability and discord to balance, cooperation, and peace. They rely on getting a large number of people into a heart/brain coherence in synchrony with the Earth's energetic and geomagnetic fields. Their sense of wholeness extends to entire populations worldwide harmonizing with the Schumann resonance generated by the Earth.[10]

Most of us don't have access to the testing and research that the Global Coherence Initiative relies on for feedback to measure global coherence. What we do have access to is our body and the feedback it provides moment by moment—when we care to notice and use its valuable information to develop our emotional, somatic, energetic, and spiritual intelligence. At your fingertips are your body's cues that you can trust and follow, not subscribing to a belief willy-nilly, but attending to what is taking place and following its flows of sensations and trails of perceptions. Notice. Feel. Be curious. Witness and become the authority of your subjective and intersubjective experience. We attend to both the obvious and—perhaps more importantly because we tend to ignore it—the subjective, subtle phenomena of the body. We shower compassion upon areas we may prefer to remain locked off. This broadened attention reveals the underlying streams operating in our body that connect to the life within and beyond our body. The amount of information available that supports integrative knowing is as endless as the currents of the ocean and the pull of the moon.

A MINDFUL APPROACH

Mindfulness, which more and more people are embracing, is key. A mindfulness practice heightens awareness of our thoughts, emotions, sensations, movements, and behaviors. Mindfulness shows the differences between helpful and unhelpful habits, behaviors that reinforce victimization and destruction, and those that lead to choice, growth, and freedom. Mindfulness shines a light into our dark, neglected regions, points out options, and reveals the appeal of authenticity, which we increasingly embrace because other actions pale in comparison. The directness of authenticity promotes connection with self and all else.

At its best, mindfulness pulls the curtain back to reveal Oz pulling levers, the face resembling ours. We are able to identify the limiting roles and perspectives and choose ones that nurture wholeness and coherence. A result of mindfulness is being present, which has inherent rewards, namely feeling connected and purposeful, all of which support the sympathetic and autonomic nervous systems working in harmony with our best interests in mind, body, energy, and spirit.

Mindfulness as it was intended includes awareness of our total being. Yet popularity and enthusiastic marketing campaigns promising quick and easy methods have contributed to it becoming a substandard practice due to poorly trained teachers overlooking the nuance, complexity, and entirety of being. Mindfulness practice may be mistaken as a concentration activity for controlling meandering and chaotic thoughts, calm being its sole objective. This may do little more than rearrange mental furniture, not shine a light on our unconscious, heighten awareness and presence, or provide insight. Additionally, if an aha moment occurs, it can leave us susceptible to its seductions, aggrandizing our ego and not contributing to authentic being or growth. Concentration is a part of mindfulness. Sensing the body and witnessing the links between thought, feeling, and action must be included. Once we're grounded in the physical body, awareness can be expanded to include the energetic and spiritual body.

Mindfulness supports the flow of the life force and welcomes acknowledging the details of the present moment. It is not pushing aside uncomfortable feelings like anger, jealousy, or confusion for an artifice of peace. This misleading version of the practice goes by the name of spiritual bypassing, which is a denial of What Is. If difficult feelings show up, we are responsive to them, welcoming them into our house but with a watchful eye, care, and a readiness to interfere should they get too unwieldy. We identify and witness the feelings, but do not blend with them. We witness the verbal and nonverbal body through softening the fascia around the heart and at the soles of our feet in resonance with the earth. If calm and peace result, it is genuine, radiant, spacious, and vitalizing.

Due to misunderstandings of the practice that mistakenly emphasize mental activity above all else, I sometimes refer to such practices as *embodied mindfulness,* a term I acknowledge is redundant. Embodied mindfulness is a reminder that any mindfulness practice worth its effort includes not only the mind but also the body and sensate awareness. The mess and lull of emotions, our flailing and victories, and the influx of energetic and spiritual phenomena are all received as welcome information. Embodied mindfulness encourages tuning in to our attitude and holding every circumstance with a degree of levity. We notice the details of our experiences, the fits and ease, and peer within, the curtain pulled back to the levers Oz has chosen. We study the self to forget the self, to loosen our binds and welcome the continuous unfolding of life.

Embodied mindfulness ties a body responsive to each moment, motion to sensation, feeling to knowing, awareness of present to presence, a marriage between past and future, all in flow. It supports establishing one's body as a welcome home regardless of circumstances. The ideal situation is always the present moment. No undo stress that raises cortisol levels. No exiling a thought. No denying an experience. By embodying all of who we are, parts known and unknown, parts existing for years and those newly peeking out, an emerging and immanence, our senses marvel at the world continually unfolding.

Here I am where I always am, in presence and appreciation, grief giving way to anger, anger giving way to joy, joy giving way to despair, despair giving way to calm, calm giving way to appreciation, looking within and outward, feeling and noticing resonance in words and wordlessness, motion and stillness, a kaleidoscope of phenomena and impressions.

Embodied mindfulness includes awareness of the field. Here is a region hidden for many of us, a result of our own doing and the culture preferring we look elsewhere. There is no elsewhere. There is only here and now, this body in confluence with all that resonates inwardly and outwardly into infinity. Perhaps details from the field appear on the screen of our attention as a vision, a change in bodily temperature, a voice, or sudden knowing. The work of our life is sensing and knowing our world, discovering wholeness, our perceptions expanding. Integrating the parts, breaking through confusion and fear and feeling how connecting to nature enervates the body, is crucial in helping us meet current existential challenges.

Just this breath. Just this feeling, this looking, this question, this word and urge, the sacredness of this moment, this attraction and distraction, this pain and where it leads, this joy and where it leads. These are the crucial steps toward a habitable future, to explore and develop ourselves, to attend to presence, to embody, to appreciate our material and energetic selves, and to integrate what is unconscious into our awareness.

Try This

Write down what you notice. Begin with obvious and subtle events of your body. Then shift your awareness to what you detect in the room. Next turn your attention beyond the room. Include what you experience with certainty, for instance, the engine rumble of a passing truck. Include more speculative perceptions, such as a cloud of fear passing on the street. Welcome the stream of your awareness without judgment.

IMAGINAL SELF

Another route toward knowing is through the imagination. It amplifies the not readily perceived material, perceptions within reach but not immediately accessible, not without effort. Imagination provides an inroad to seemingly opposing worlds, functioning like the corpus callosum that ensures one side of the brain transmits information to the other. There is the self we know that makes its appearance daily and the one tiptoeing in the periphery of awareness. Your job is to bring this reluctant and obscured part forward for self-knowing and integration, to applaud abilities that uphold the status quo and, equally important, the uncommon ones needed for buttressing wholeness.

Imagination is often discounted as child's play, make-believe, a superfluous activity. Far from it. Rather, it is a treasure trove of information, fertile territory for contemplation, the wings that launch thought, a crack in the surface that reveals a stratum of perception.

Imagination points to a subterranean world operating beyond view. It is a type of communication that abides by its own set of rules, a logic with a nonlinear potency. If discounting imagination is our modus operandi, we lose out on the wily way it contributes to knowledge, insight, and somatic and energetic intelligence. We overlook a significant cache of information.

Imagination arrives like a beacon cutting through a cloud to offer a way. It is a leap into another time and space . . . which is present. It is this feeling and all that is this moment but refigured. It's how ideas, emotions, and sensations assume perceptible form that may include image, language, movement, or sound. Imagination uses the language of dream, abstraction, symbolism, analogy, association, and conflation, any one of these slippery. Of utmost importance, imagination is the key that unlocks the door to the unconscious and provides entry to this frequently hidden vital room. Episcopal priest Cynthia Bourgeault recognizes the imagination as occupying its own realm. Referring to it as the imaginal, she describes it as a confluence or "meeting ground, a place of active exchange between two bandwidths of reality . . . realms invisible but still perceivable through the eye of the heart."[11]

Imagination supports liberties that literal thinking leaves behind. It enables us to enter the hidden room to look around, to touch the furniture, to poke our finger through a slot in the bird cage, the details not literal, but suggestive, analogous, allowing us to establish connections. Not only does this way of thinking launch new thought, but it sails it across an ocean or enters a black hole to recover parts of us awaiting claim and integration. Perhaps the words on this page prompted you to shift your feet upon the floor, or they led you to lift your gaze out the window skyward to recall your stellar alchemy, that we are, as astrophysicist Carl Sagan said, "made of star stuff."[12] Perhaps you can feel or imagine the flux of the cosmos within.

Imagination recognizes that an idea is rarely only one thing but wears multiple guises. Consider the idea of love. Imagine it. Let it launch an image. Invite the feeling into your body. Let the feeling well up from wherever it lives. Witness what manifests. Watch how you limit yourself or let go. Whatever took place was your imagination in play, vague or clear, with blurred edges or distinct lines.

What would happen if we imagined with heart, with embodied mindfulness, with an awareness of the energetic field in the tension of opposition and in the trust of flow? What would happen if we released ourselves from the prison of limiting beliefs to face all of who we are, who not, and who we could be? What new patterns emerge?

What is encountered is bodying the myriad ways of perceiving this moment. We encounter language and idea in play. We encounter us in motion and motion moving us. We encounter our growing and growth itself. There is nothing there, we conclude. Or this nothing is everything. Imagine your voice echoing across a canyon. Imagine others similarly hollering perched at the edge, an intermingle of voices colliding in the near distance.

Bodying and self-knowing reveal themselves as endless processes. Self-knowing is the very route to what lies within and beyond self. Holding it lightly and examining our life spawns a joy that is purposeful and purposeless, breath its own reason for being, appreciating beauty reason enough, feeling love reason enough, experiencing awe reason enough. What emerges is an intrinsic joy and deep peace, a unity with self that influences every other relationship with family, friends, colleagues, the biotic and abiotic world, the perceptible and imperceptible, a grand dance of atoms and cells. What emerges are the sorrows and joys that solicit a deep union and a return to what is fundamental.

When we let the body speak. When we let the heart and gut open to deep breath. When we attend to what rouses curiosity. When we center in being. When we follow energy. When looking within is looking out. When what we judged as impossible becomes possible.

Writing is a continual coming out, an emerging of self, a revelation and disclosure on the line. As it is with dancing, except it is a moving body that reveals the process of creating, the unmanifest assuming form. As it is with meditating when stillness vibrates subtle motion. As it is with walking or standing or running with open awareness switched on. Every moment is a turning point for innermost experiences and ongoing awareness. Every moment is collaborating with the continual unfolding of creation. Every moment the trees and soil and lakes and longing join forces.

EXPANDING CONSCIOUSNESS

Mindful embodiment inevitably leads to expanded perceptions. The stream of sensations becomes increasingly detectable to the point that we rely on them for valuable information of internal and external conditions, the muscle of awareness strengthening and becoming more agile. We hear an unfathomable silence. We shiver from an ineffable nuance. We glimpse a promising vision of tomorrow. We become aware of the necessity of language to say what needs saying. We become aware, too, of the deficits of language, words supplemented by motion and stillness. In place is awe abiding with What Is, always on the verge, always in process, the intelligence of the body, a life force operating within and beyond our control. Its color is transparent, its shape amorphous, its sound a hum, its word a poem exact in its inexactitude.

Expanding consciousness enlarges the frame, a few filters swapped out or removed altogether. It supports a recognition of continuity, unity and collaboration, a coherence of beauty with a heart in full vibratory beating, its pulse quickening life nearby as itself is quickened. Here is inspiration. Here are viable solutions. Here is a body reckoning with all of life. Here is the opportunity to right imbalances with breath, surrender, intuition, feminism, patriarchy, boldness, empathy, hurt, forgiveness, innovation, speaking up, listening, walking, planting, planning, dying, birthing, knowing, unknowing, and trusting. Not one or another but science and intuition, reason and imagination, familiar perceptions and those in the hinterlands of consideration.

In the process, inner and outer world in and out of focus, we touch the core of authentic selfing, embodying, the body continually in revision. The hints, hunches, and intuitions in and out of time, from the space of the body and its field is our multidimensionality. Our physical and energetic body and the ongoing stream of sensory experience broadens imagination, reveals connections, and sends out new threads, purifying our folly and clarifying meaning. Wholeness becomes possible through noticing the cascade of impressions. We are not apart from experience, but experience itself, being always on the threshold of becoming. We are not apart from nature, but nature itself. We are because the earth is. You are as I am.

We are made of the same material as shadows. We murmur along with trees, rocks, and fungus. A despairing heart repairs itself. Breath provides sutures. An open mind is a staircase to the stars.

What can take place at such junctures is an altered consciousness, the world as we knew it or believed possible arranging itself anew. We may get disoriented. We may lose balance, our center off-kilter. Our familiar paradigm ruptures as if we finally find the volume button after years of the remote stuck on mute. An adjacent button turns on inner sight, spatial awareness, proprioception, intuition, remote viewing, and other underutilized perceptual channels. Now with greater force than before, sound waves press upon our eardrum, light touches the optic nerve, and receptors in the skin startle the senses. This unfamiliar, bewildering stretch and attentiveness is the very process required in recovering a balance, an adjustment to the emergence of a new paradigm.

Psychologist Arnold Mindell explains altered consciousness as switching from a common perceptual channel to one infrequently used, hence the disorientation. It's as if a new operating system is installed, the apps and files moved, and we must learn the changed steps to access information. Disorientation is a knock at the door of the senses and a call, if we're up to it, to integrate the new experience. An altered state cracks the shell of a limited perception as a new awareness pokes through, one we hope lands us safely on both feet. Mystifying, mundane, frightening, ecstatic, or reassuring, such new possibilities reveal being as porous and multidimensional, expanding upon what we thought was possible.

Here lies a more spacious, genuine, empowered intimacy with all that is. Here lies an invisible network of life. Here lie authentic, vibrant being, and radiant awareness. Straightforward and subtle, manifest and obscure, palpable and imaginal distinctions shift, blend, and continually reform. Integral philosopher Ken Wilber sees these as transcendent mystical experiences that "re-orient awareness to an opening of new and higher states of consciousness, including a direct sense of oneness with the entire universe . . . one is waking up to a pure, transparent, open, empty, clear awareness, free of incoherent and broken thoughts and frameworks . . . sometimes referred to as discovering your highest Self, your True Self, your Real Condition."[13]

As consciousness alters, we exist in a between state, an unfamiliar and unsettling liminal place, not quite here or there, one foot in dream, the other in awakening; one foot in a familiar paradigm, the other in a nascent, uncommon one. These liminal places support a type of indigenous knowing familiar to shamans who travel between worlds with the ease of wind. Here something altogether new emerges. Here is growth caught in the act, a seed activated, the stem breaking through the surface, the bud in bloom. Here is an emergence, a repatterning, a poiesis of consciousness, a startle of information and perception. We follow the hunch, the strange pull, the compelling vision as if a charismatic stranger waves at us to follow. We go, senses heightened. We go, the glaze on our eyes removed. We go, the body still, another part of us roaming free. With body in deep quietude, the nervous system settled, earth and sky penetrate our being. This emergence is a crucial pivot, an orientation in disorientation, a crucible for balance. Breathe, ground, be curious.

Try This

What is taking place with your breath and energy this moment? Notice what you notice. Try something untried that beckons your attention.

Perhaps we learn a more efficient way to till the soil, or we take up journaling. Perhaps we partake in a visionary or unitary experience. Perhaps we discover the benefits of stillness. Perhaps we celebrate drinking water free of contaminants from the well in our backyard fed by the aquifer. Perhaps we eat the dandelion leaves from the yard and witness what we previously considered a weed become a source of nutrition.

Respecting each moment births a consciousness, an embrace and realization of our wholeness that is a natural progression of life. To sense heartfully with the fullness of our body acknowledges and generates transformations always taking place within and outside the margins of awareness. The world is ready. We are ready. Turbulence and discord are a prime, fertile moment to awaken. It's up to each of us to see beyond our myopic understanding, to respect all life and breathe with Earth. It's a choice made each moment.

6

A Way Forward

Perhaps a new revelatory experience is taking place, an experience wherein human consciousness awakens to the grandeur and sacred quality of the Earth process.

THOMAS BERRY

By now, you've spent some time tuning in to your body and biofield to broaden and refine your awareness, discoveries lending themselves to a shift underway. The path of embodied presence and expanded awareness rewards with each moment. Perseverance with the path results in change toward thriving.

The word *thriving* is simple enough. It means to grow, develop, or prosper. Thriving is what's taking place with my neighbor's garden that gets full sun and produces a bounty of raspberries, peaches, tomatoes, chard, and asparagus. Thriving is what is taking place with my friend's ten-year-old son, who switched from a school where he showed little interest and was failing to a school that captures his attention and motivation. Thriving is what can take place when needs are taken care of without worry about health, food, employment, and climate.

To focus on thriving is not only to survive, but to tap into the abundance of the universe and the perseverance of the generative life pulse. We continue. Life goes on. Cells divide and increase in size and shape. Seeds rise up from or fall to the ground and germinate. Flood waters recede and parched land hydrates. Life is propelled by sun, water, air, and food. Thriving welcomes one step after another carrying out DNA instructions and helped along with factors in the environment. Thriving implies flourishing and suggests that everything is going well.

Thriving is as palpable as the morning's first gulp of water quenching our dry throat. Being resonates with thriving without succumbing to wishful thinking or grasping at empty promises. We feel it in our bones, in our heart, in our breath, and in the calm of our gut. We don't avoid what makes us uncomfortable, the despair, guilt, grief, and powerlessness in the face of cataclysmic circumstances. But as or more important, we feel the coexistence of inspiration, joy, beauty, and resilience. All feelings are essential to acknowledge if we are to evolve and take actions to bring about needed change to ensure a hospitable planet.

We may decide to focus upon thriving and need to revisit the idea multiple times for it to take hold. A subscription to thriving is not automatically renewed, especially if a previous habit works against it. Habits are broken through vigilant attention and compassion. Circumstances continually test our resolve and provide ample time to practice the new behavior. A preferred outcome requires a commitment.

On the surface, my client Richard has an ideal life: a wife, two children, a dog, a paid-off house in the suburbs, regular trips to visit extended family, two vacations per year, and good physical health. He came to me with chronic depression. When he spoke about his life, he rattled off a list of complaints about how his dog pulled on his arm during walks, his wife insisted upon getting together with her girlfriends on weekends, and he had to take time out of his busy week to pack for going away. Despite what appeared to be a stable life, he framed the details of his week negatively and predicted that it would remain difficult. "What would make it better?" I asked. "What would it look like?"

After a long pause, he replied that he didn't know. Working on him revealed a gray field that felt depleted and was held stubbornly close to his body. After our sessions, he reported feeling more relaxed, which he welcomed, yet the negativity persisted. When I suggested he see a therapist or doctor to get a prescription for depression, he said he did not see how it would help. "Nah," he said with characteristic brevity to my query, his thinking and brain chemistry closed to change.

MULTIPLE PERSPECTIVES

It takes effort, sometimes great effort, to upend a habit and unplug the default of a self-sabotaging program, especially one that's been running for years, one that reinforces complacency. Familiarity with a set of beliefs may erroneously cause us to equate it with reality and we don't see our bias or, in Richard's case, a filter cemented into place.

I'm reminded of a Chinese parable about a farmer and his commiserating townspeople. One day, a farmer's horse ran away. The townspeople visited the farm to offer condolences. "So sorry for your loss," they said.

"We'll see," replied the farmer.

The following day, the horse returned with several wild horses. "Lucky you," said the townspeople.

"We'll see," replied the farmer.

The farmer's son went to ride one of the horses, got thrown to the ground, and broke his leg. "So sorry," said the townspeople.

"We'll see," said the farmer.

The next week, war broke out and officers came searching for able young men to enlist as soldiers. The son's broken leg exempted him from military duty. "Lucky you," said the townspeople.

The parable reveals how any one circumstance can be viewed multiple ways depending on where we end the story. No situation can be so neatly defined as positive or negative. The parable challenges any hasty assessment and reinforces the idea that any event is more complex than initially perceived.

Admittedly, to thrive is a filter, but it's one that works on our behalf. It reinforces resilience and growth. It suggests adherence to a dynamic balance, adapting and persisting, taking action and allowing. We learn a new skill. We identify the source of a sensation. We wrestle with and understand an emotion. We align with grace. We do the work that needs to be done. We look within and outside ourselves. To thrive means that growth is taking place—which may be physical, emotional, mental, or spiritual. We may take up a new hobby or let go of one. We may seek a new job or return to school. We may begin to use the bus instead of a car or join a group that works toward creating a policy that improves water quality. Upon uncovering the source of negativity, we can then uproot it and adopt actions that work on our behalf. Genuine growth makes visible differences between how we were before and how we are now.

In some ways, with so many systems failing and too many of us suffering, a focus on thriving may seem inappropriate. But it's exactly the right time because breakdowns and broken systems are a call to action that demands rethinking and repair. The time is now to no longer take conditions for granted nor loiter in complacency and instead to extend a hand, gaze, or idea to activate a dormant potential and creative solution that respects and protects nature.

Thriving encourages examining and altering thinking and behavior, especially any harmful pattern. The focus is on staying present and cultivating what is working, which supports our interest and tosses out what falls short or works against us. It's a choice much like the choice to love. Everything may not be all right in this moment, but investing in what is working carries us forward. A focus on thriving enables us to identify the route and necessary steps. In doing so, a setback can be transformed into an opportunity and a loss into a gain. Obstacles, however minor or egregious, can be regarded as temporary and reveal themselves as opportunities. New behaviors and approaches are tried. We attend to what's been ignored. We allow pain to transform us. We reframe an idea, explore, and learn. We open to our senses and intuition. We experience the awe of life unfolding and measure progress. Everything, we soon find out, is both all right and not all right, and we have the intelligence and wherewithal to disrupt a harmful process for a beneficial one. The story continues until a workable, acceptable conclusion is reached, a harmful behavior corrected.

Holding the idea of thriving in mind is a significant part of the equation. The idea becomes a plausible aim. The very action of holding it in mind sets up the likelihood for it to manifest given our body's responsiveness to our thoughts. Writer Joe Dispenza finds that there's more working behind the scenes and beneath the skin than is detectable in any moment. He says, "Every time you have a thought there is a biochemical reaction in the brain."[1] The content of those thoughts releases corresponding chemicals that make us feel uplifted or anxious, empowered or discouraged. What we are feeling also prompts a biochemical reaction that then leads to corresponding thoughts.

Every thought and feeling matters more than we may give them credit for. We are both producer and product, the finger knocking over the domino and the tile knocked over. What we think influences how we feel as much as what we feel influences what we think. Both influence perceptions and a willingness to take actions. To maintain what works, change our world, and thrive, it helps to monitor the content of our thoughts and cultivate the ones with our best interests at heart. Mindful presence to the content of our thoughts and consequent actions provide inroads to balance, power, and a habitable future.

EMBODYING GROWTH

Thinking is part of the equation. As significant is feeling and embodying thriving. Seeing may be believing but feeling goes further. It enables us to feel reality not tomorrow, which is an abstraction, but now. We touch the flesh and pulse of the body. We sense a contraction and release in our belly. We anchor attention and investigate surface and depth. We employ awareness and perceptions without thought taking us away. What results is a joyful glow filling our body creating its own momentum. The feedback from sensing places us in coherence with self and surroundings. It keeps us in touch with the fuel that turns an idea into reality and supports functioning from our highest potential.

Somatic and energetic components show the body in process, thriving already underway. Nothing is staid, which means that each conscious and unconscious decision turns us toward or away from thriving. It's up to us. Now. With this breath, the way we look out the window and hold this book in hand. With the mind that reflects our willingness to listen to ourselves, one another, and the universe. Not denying or ignoring but acknowledging. Attending. Listening somatically and ecosomatically. Our somatic intelligence, the knowing that comes from intimately connecting to our personal body, reveals the thoughts and feelings we welcome and those that get pushed aside, pivotal information for maintaining our current course or altering direction. Our energetic intelligence reveals the degree to which we consider and engage the subtle flows, light, vibration, and the biofield, all containing pivotal information. Ecosomatic listening recognizes that attending to our personal body includes also attending to the planetary body.

Below is a list of ideas I associate with thriving. They're set up in two columns to emphasize their differences. A given situation may require more of one than the other, however, thriving ultimately necessitates a focus on one with an eye toward the other, hence my emphasis on "and."

personal	and	interpersonal
intrapersonal	and	communal
somatic	and	energetic
outer senses	and	inner senses

known	and	emergent
grounded	and	heart centered
receiving	and	giving
reflecting	and	taking action
sensory based	and	intuitive
reason	and	imagination
single perspective	and	multiple perspectives
individualistic	and	collective
unilateral	and	collaborative
masculine	and	feminine
anthropocentric	and	ecocentric
biocentric	and	cosmocentric

Thriving is an ongoing awareness and commitment to a process. The process taps into flow, fullness, and resourcefulness. It supports being nimble enough in body and mind to take appropriate action. It points to celebrating and believing in ourselves and others despite limitations. Connection and interdependence are valued as the very essence of the life current.

An element of thriving is developing and pursuing curiosity. The area of curiosity that warrants developing varies person to person.

Try This

Make a list of the ways you are thriving and the areas that fall short. In reviewing your list, look for patterns that correspond to strengths but also weaknesses. A weakness may indicate an area that is calling for attention.

Many of us tend to pursue areas of strengths and ignore areas of weakness. There's good reason to use strengths. They reinforce competence and make use of abilities toward the smooth running of our day. They provide satisfaction and make us feel valuable. But there's also good reason to explore and utilize weaknesses. Learning something new establishes new synaptic paths, making our brain and the rest of us more durable. Mind and thinking are refreshed and spark ideas. They contribute to attaining a goal and moving on to consequent ones. They reinforce the confidence and satisfaction that comes from self-reliance and increase consciousness.

Competence in a strength area fans the ego, yet for the sake of development, I encourage exploring a weak area. Every intelligence provides a unique set of tools for perceiving. An ability in one area can be applied elsewhere and provide a missing piece, shaping connections between areas that initially appear unrelated. For instance, a naturalist intelligence, the ability to observe and understand nature, gets us to notice changing water levels in a marsh and how this wetland is pivotal to minimizing erosion. It allows us to understand how foods like apples and broccoli rely on pollinating bees. An understanding of marshes and pollination may lead to developing a trash interceptor or a vaccine. It may provide a potent metaphor that provokes the mind to leap between ideas to forge a vital connection. It favors relaxing a tendency to specialize and categorize for crossing boundaries for merging disciplines and developing new ideas.

Along these lines is the value of identifying your primary way of perceiving, your perspective, and finding another perspective to explore, at its core a pivotal creative process. Shift whatever part of yourself you readily identify with. For instance, what information is available to you when you read these words as a global citizen instead of as an employee? Or rather than identifying yourself as the subject, see yourself as the object. What information comes to the foreground when you imagine your neighbor looking upon your life? How does your pet see you? How does a tree or stream experience you? What happens when the biofield influences you?

Entertaining multiple perspectives moves us out of the bias of our perspective into greater knowing. We experience the expansion where the many dimensions of being and knowing meet. We end up listening to bodying and to the living Earth. We encounter an energetic union, the intermingling of interconnection. We discover our body as familiar and unfamiliar, our inquiry continually placing the edge of our limits further and further afield while also riding on our attention.

You and me and us as them. Air as breath and soil as home. A new way of seeing and sensing. A map of hope, health, and resilience.

Entertaining multiple perspectives supports identifying themes and patterns in our life, refining who we are, and maturing. We get to nurture what longs to emerge, a nascent ability awaiting its turn. We can retire what no longer works in favor of what does. We can undo the harm foisted upon us by family, school, and culture and cultivate qualities and interests that are sustainable and embrace the best of who we are. We can toss out self-defeating behavior to free up living to the potential of the greater good of which we are an intrinsic part.

We pursue such activities because genuine growth is mutually beneficial. Thriving depends on working with systems be they physiological, ecological, or energetic. Thriving recognizes that genuine growth takes place amid air, sun, family, community, and the biofield. Any one action prompts other responses and actions in subtle and obvious ways. Consider the impact of a smile. Consider the impact of encouraging versus discouraging words. Consider the impact of a well-intentioned touch which calms, lowers blood pressure, reduces inflammation, and increases oxytocin levels and overall health, among the reasons caregivers are encouraged to reach out as is appropriate with patients.[2] Consider investigating a glimmer at the outskirts of your awareness.

We pursue such actions because something within spurs us on and we've learned to trust the nudges and glimpses from intuition and the wisdom of the body. We pursue them because going beyond personality and culture reaches toward something deeper within us that is core to the well-being of personal, collective, and planetary health. We step onto the edge of knowing, awareness blowing our hair and opening a gate of the mind. Learning is within reach.

Thriving invigorates. The untamed, unknown, invisible world rises up to our senses. Passivity meets activity. Part of us speaks as another listens. Reaching out is a reaching within. The world enchants and surprises with its every expression, with how the wind howls, an engine rumbles, and a log floats downriver. We are enchanted with the sound of a friend's voice and the music of silence.

When thriving, we are accessing and engaging the flux of creation. The act of creating, be it for art, commerce, or an environmental project, taps into the fundamental workings of the universe, which is continually connecting, configuring, and transmuting. Each moment births a thought, a book, a chair, a tadpole, a stream, a cloud. By consciously participating in each moment, awareness tuned to its unfolding, the veil between worlds lifts and we see the steps underfoot and ahead. Visible is how one action and event leads to another, be it seed into a harvest, rain into flooding, or despair into an evolutionary shift.

This active participation reveals details everywhere, in the stretch of our fingers, in the completion of an exhalation, in how we say hello, body ourselves, and look outward. Presence reveals itself in absence, stillness in motion, a gift in sorrow. We step back from our life to be in step with life and to better know ourselves and another. We perch on the crest of a mountain among lightning bugs. We listen to the shrill call of cicadas. We walk toward the edge of the familiar because something about being present to the usual and the unusual nourishes us in an uncanny way. Something we hadn't noticed before now enlivens us, every phenomenon containing the potential to reveal some new marvel.

Where we've been links us to what wants to emerge and urges action. Looking ahead helps along with sensing our feet meeting the ground and our gaze looking a few steps ahead. We stay present to

What Is: this word, this memory, this pain, this curiosity, this root, this stone, this storm, this hope, this need.

If fear arises, we recognize its appearance and do what may be needed to mitigate harm, but we do not let it hold us back. The rapid heartbeat or torpor teaches us about our body. The mind's chatter teaches us how to use breath for adjusting the volume. We step boldly with a watchful eye. We watch how imagination, intuition, the song of a robin, the rumble of thunder, despair, and hope wake us up. We take a chance and let chance take us.

BREAKING THROUGH

Thriving transforms a setback into a breakthrough, a tension into a release. An opening develops where previously there was none. We work toward hitting a stride and establishing a flow. The subtleties and intricacies of the moment captivate us, the light falling on the desk, our jaw clenching and unclenching, the scurry to jot down a note, the need to make our voice heard, and take meaningful action. The narrow focus provides a freedom that simultaneously links to a broader view and deeper breath. What lies beneath, above, and beyond is always more than our eyes can see and our hands can reach, yet we extend ourselves anyway.

Connections, always available, bring us home to the body. We are conscious of how we move and what moves us. We recognize the world making us and us making the world. We attend to the events arising each moment, some arriving seemingly from nowhere, others easily trackable. All are worthy of our attention and reinforce consciously connecting, an awakening continually in process that involves us living from our depths, from the hidden and visible, from mystery and dream, and nudges that beckon. "Look here," it says. "Follow this." And we do because the extraordinary complexity of the world is always with us, is us, if only we would sit, stand, walk, look, feel, remember, and take the time to consider the body as matter and energy, temple and field, an intermingling of you and everyone and everything else, too vast for any one page or mind.

Thriving is connected to evolutionary change. It touches into the core of who we are and to the pulse of life. Thriving welcomes stasis, homeostasis, and growth, alert to cycles of breath, of cell formation, of social and political trends, of layers of soil and atmosphere, of people who come into our life and depart, of periods of hardship and periods of ease.

Thriving is connected to an evolution of consciousness. Consciousness grows through reflection and practices that recognize What Is while also challenging the status quo. Sense, accept, and question. It grows by moving the body and the mind. It grows by answering the knock at the door of awareness and tending to the needs of me and you. It grows by learning how to engage in reciprocity with friend, stranger, nature, and nurture. It grows by feeling deeply into the physical, energetic, and ecological body that is ours and finding the body we did not recognize as ours.

Thriving positions us on a personal and collective edge welcoming transformation. Just this moment. Here, now, with these perfect and ever-shifting conditions, a recognition, too, about how we've been influenced and conditioned. What does it take to get out of our own way? What does it take to activate the self we always knew ourselves to be for the world dreamed possible? What does it take to balance at the enigmatic edge with the scintillating energy of our body as home contributing to the delivery of a welcome future? What does it take to wake up the dormant abilities that make today and tomorrow more livable?

Thriving involves personal and collective well-being in connection to the natural world, a necessary inclusion. The prosperity of an individual extends to the prosperity of a group, which extends to the health of the entire ecological community as evidenced in the COVID pandemic and climate disruption. Harm to another harms us; assisting another helps us. Genuine thriving recognizes that supporting one body supports all bodies.

Locating where thriving lives in your body leads to actions that can be taken to keep the heat glowing enough to warm the body and animate the mind for the sake of yourself, your family, and the planet. Look to sense what occupies your awareness and what hovers on the outskirts. Feel the suppleness of knowing that is susceptible to change with each consequent moment. The self-disclosure shows how we dwell with our body, how we look within and to the horizon, how everything we encounter carries a promise that welcomes our care. In us opening to the world, the world reveals its splendors.

In thinking about the future, I consider what my family and friends might say of me. I'd like them to say I was among those who supported an era of awakening.

If you haven't already done so, this is the point in the book when you look out the window into yourself. Not just looking, but feeling with the cells, respiration, and inspiration. This is when the heart radiates, the mind dances, and silence reveals the footsteps of earth. When energy activates and inner lights turn on. When constricted muscles release to an embodied presence and the gate to a new awareness swings wide.

7

Embodiment Practices

This section of the book invites you to explore and further develop your awareness and perceptions. Of upmost importance is attending closely to your sensory, energetic, intuitive, and imaginal self. Tune in to the obvious but also the subtle details of awareness that typically escape notice, the ones you might otherwise readily discount. It's up to you to touch into the field of your being. Watch for what shows up and what slips away. Be documentarian, adventurer, anthropologist, witness, expert, novice, seeker, and friend. Blaze a trail into yourself. Follow clues. Commit to embodying the dynamic flux of presence.

The exercises point out a way to learn about yourself. Ultimately the best method is your practice and the best authority is you: your sensing, intuiting, imagining, and reasoning. You engaging your abilities and developing new ones. You intending, planning, and letting go. You aligning with the present moment that grounds you in homecoming, renewal, expansion. This pivotal initial step will assist you in getting to know the patterns and anomalies of your being. Track the patterns of perceptions and behaviors along with any exceptions. Assume responsibility as best as possible by acting from a place of wholeness.

What follows are several practices. Give yourself the attention and depth of listening and feeling you crave. Welcome the investigation. Go further than thought. Let yourself dream. Let yourself be guided by the unknown. Be curious. Loosen your usual parameters, especially any perfectionist tendencies to get it right. Sometimes the best learning takes place through tangents and mistakes. Give yourself generous leeway for exploring. Journal or draw about what takes place if you want. Practicing bodily intelligence and expanded perceptions is an ongoing commitment and journey.

Consider skimming over the practices before deciding which one to do first. Do them sequentially or in your preferred order. Several reap better results when repeated.

Setting Intentions

Frequency: as needed
Objective: for clarity and manifestation

Before you engage with any of the practices in the following pages of this chapter, I urge you to articulate your intention, preferably in writing. Intentions focus attention and shift energy. More than a to-do list, they get the entire body on board and transmit their message to the universe.

o Define an intention. Be as specific as possible with choice words. For example, *I am being more patient and compassionate with myself. I am letting go of my habit of self-criticism.* The "I am-ing" sets the action in the present and reinforces it already taking place.

o As you form the intention, notice its resonance in your body. Where and how do you feel it?

o Imagine the intention echoing throughout your body. See how the intention takes up space within.

o Expand your intention to the field immediately surrounding your body. Watch how it begins just beyond your skin and emanates farther out. Feel your body as awareness of the field expands. Trust that the seed of your intention is planted.

o Let go of your focus and turn your attention to the associated practice.

Initiating a Practice

Frequency: periodically

Objective: to initiate a practice

Option: to be done alone or with a group

These generalized prompts are intended to get you started with a practice. I purposefully left them open-ended to see what they instigate. Any one of these could take minutes, weeks, or months to do. Which elicits excitement, fear, avoidance, and inspiration? Consider your reactions to be helpful information.

o Discover beauty. Look around you or create it.

o Embody yourself. Focus awareness on any part of your body. Rest your hands on a part of your body.

o Imagine. Use sound, images, and motion. Let them arise from the corners of your awareness.

o Trust flow. Follow your curiosity. Follow confusion. Follow doubt, grief, excitement, or whatever else shows up. Follow what calls your attention.

o Feel what your body is communicating.

o Attend mindfully. Notice what you notice and what you dismiss.

o Breathe slowly, fully, and easily as if this activity is paramount— as if the sunrise depends on it.

o Question. Listen with the entirety of your body, sense into situations, and investigate.

o Relax. Stretch your body. Take up more space.

o Consult with skilled practitioners. Notice how your experience is similar and different.

o Integrate. Use your experiences to foster self-acceptance and growth. Become intimate with yourself and with systems larger than yourself.

Shining a Light for Integration

Frequency: once or periodically

Objective: to define weak and disavowed parts of ourselves for strengthening and integration

Identifying weak and disavowed parts brings them into awareness, acceptance, and reframing. The new awareness allows us to understand them differently and claim them as playing an important role in who we have been or are.

o Make a list of areas of your life that give you pride, resilience, and satisfaction. This could be activities, beliefs, and accomplishments. To get you going, you can use the prompt, "I feel good about . . . "

o Make the list fifty items long. Be honest, forthright, and generous in your appraisal.

o As you record each item, notice what pride, resilience, and satisfaction feel like in your body.

o Reflect on each one. Congratulate and honor yourself in some way. This could be something as simple as smiling or feeling gratitude.

o Now make a second list of areas of your life that make you feel shame. It may be parts that you prefer others did not know about. To get you going, you can use the prompt, "I feel uneasy about . . . "

o Keep this list short, anywhere between five and ten items long.

o Notice your bodily feeling and thoughts as you record each item. Notice, for instance, your reluctance or eagerness to write it down or how your heart hardens. Gently allow feelings to rise up.

o Congratulate yourself for your honesty.

o Choose an item from the second list that you are willing to investigate.

o Write about an event (or events) that contributed to your shame. If you prefer, you can also draw a picture. If there were people involved with this event, who were they and what were their actions? What were the circumstances that led to belittling conclusions about yourself?

o Give yourself compassion for the shame or any other unsettling emotions. Place your hands on your heart. Breathe easily.

o Imagine that a mature version of yourself is giving wise counsel and comfort to a younger you. Or imagine what you would say to a best friend who has confided in you and wants your support. Be generous in the support you give to yourself.

o Notice sensations. Where in your body does the feeling arise or feel stuck?

o What action can you take toward self-compassion and understanding to bring this area of yourself to the light of wholeness? Come up with five possibilities, some easily doable with yourself and some with someone you trust. Plan to do one within the week.

o Seek the support of a friend, family member, or professional for additional help if needed.

o When ready, go through the same process with another item on your list.

Transforming Fear and Worry into Love

Frequency: as needed

Objective: to increase the presence and power of love, reduce constriction, and reinforce connection

Worry alerts us to something being off balance. Ongoing worry without consequent action can be harmful. Engaging love reinforces support from others, the life force, and provides the impetus to right a situation.

o You can do this seated or lying down.

o Place your hands restfully on your heart. You can use both hands if that feels more comfortable. Feel the heat or cool or any other sensation.

o Close your eyes to increase inner awareness. Follow your attention or the dream of your awareness.

o Invite compassion and love to engage with the energy of your heart. Give these feelings a color or symbolic image or see what arises on its own.

o Choose something that is frightening or worrisome.

o Invite the fear or worry to engage with the energy of your heart. Imagine it dipping into the liquid of your heart and watch the dilution. Or imagine the waves of the heart breaking it apart.

o Focus on gently breathing at the heart. Feel its flow, waves, or any other sensation.

o Imagine the sensation emanating beyond the heart to your entire chest and body, creating a field of love and compassion. Allow its soothing energy to fill your body, going so far as to fill the trillion cells of your being. Do this for several minutes.

o Invite the field to expand however far it wants to go, just outside the perimeter of your body or perhaps filling the room and moving beyond its walls.

o Allow flow. Let go of the need to control the experience. Notice what sensations, feelings, and thoughts arise. Greet all with loving energy. Be a witness.

o Luxuriate in breathing.

o Open your eyes.

o You might want to write down or draw what has taken place.

o End by standing with both feet firmly on the floor and arms easily hanging at your sides.

o What follow-up action comes to mind? What behavioral changes or activities are prompted?

Embodying through Meditation

Frequency: This exercise is most effective when done on a regular basis, preferably at the same time of day. Start small with five minutes. As it becomes more familiar, extend the time to ten, then fifteen, and twenty minutes.

Objective: to increase awareness and embodiment for grounding and developing somatic intelligence

Option: to be done alone or with a group

Meditation seems to slow time and reveal our habitual sensory reactions to situations. This information provides the option of new responses.

o Set a timer.

o Use a chair, meditation cushion, or the floor.

o Get into a comfortable, seated position with your spine elongated, chest open, with your arms easily at your side or on your lap. Notice how which part of your body is contacting the floor, cushion, or chair.

o Take in several deep breaths.

o Invite the energy of your breath into your sacrum.

o Invite the energy of your breath into your belly.

o Invite the energy of your breath into your upper chest, shoulders, and neck.

o Invite the energy of your breath into your head.

o Relax your jaw.

o Do micromovements, small adjustments that keep you in a movement flow. The size of these movements may or may not be visible to another. Do what increases your sense of spaciousness. Enjoy, play, be relaxed, and be curious.

o Notice feelings, sensations, and thoughts. Follow your attention and what shows up.

o Follow where your body leads.

o When the timer goes off, return to stillness.

o Open your eyes.

o You may want to write about or draw something that took place.

Balancing Feminine and Masculine Energies

Frequency: once or periodically

Objective: to cultivate new abilities, reclaim disowned feelings and behaviors, and reinforce balance for well-being

We are all a blend of male and female energies, yet it's likely that social conditioning caused us to ignore a vital part of us. Be vigilant with your assumptions.

o Using two pieces of paper, make a list of your qualities that you associate with being masculine on one piece of paper and feminine on the other.

o Go to the shorter list and consider a quality to add. If the lists are the same length, skip to the next step.

o Notice what feelings, sensations, and thoughts arise in the process. Watch for bias and resistance.

o Place both papers on the floor and stand upon one. While standing, imagine that you embody only those qualities on the paper. Notice what feelings, sensations, and thoughts arise in the process.

o Do the same with the second piece of paper.

o Which paper gave you more energy or less? More confusion or less? What emotion is provoked? What else did you notice?

o Stack the papers and stand upon both. Notice what feelings, sensations, and thoughts arise. What, if anything, feels out of balance?

o Notice hasty rejecting or reactivity, which suggests an area to explore further.

o How, if at all, might you revise the lists?

o How, if at all, are you ignoring your authentic self?

Healing with Imagery

Frequency: once or a few times a day
Objective: to reinforce strength and healing

The body recognizes the power of images and symbols that work upon us consciously and unconsciously. What's important with the specific images is that they have a positive personal association.

o Identify a site of your body that needs healing and place attention there using your inner senses. For emotions and thoughts, choose a site if there is no specific region.

o Rest your attention there. You might also want to place your hands on the area.

o Watch for sensations and feelings. What does the unhealed site feel like? What associations come to mind?

o Ask your body for a literal or symbolic image that is instrumental to your healing. Use your imagination as needed.

o As if lucid dreaming, engage with the image. Carry out a positive healing action that the image suggests. For instance, if a drum appears, find out what sound it makes. Continue with the story of the image until you reach a satisfying conclusion.

o Rest in the knowledge that healing properties have been activated.

o Write about or draw what has taken place.

Developing Intuition

Frequency: weekly or as wanted

Objective: to learn to trust the information that arrives intuitively and use it to expand awareness and provide information about a situation

Intuition requires practice in order to recognize the difference between fantasy and actual information. Intuition provides warnings, urgings, and other messages not readily available through common sensory channels.

o Sit quietly in a pleasing, stress-free environment with your eyes closed.

o Focus on breath for a few minutes. Notice how your chest and belly expand and contract. Is the movement fast or slow, smooth or uneven?

o Invite calm. Imagine it as a color or a memory of a location where you previously experienced calm. Feel it. Notice any other sensory events.

o Ask a question for which you want insight.

o Continue to sit while noticing any sensory events. Look for sensation, imagery, a voice, or impressions, however vague they may be. A response may be immediate, hours later, or arrive in a dream.

o Option: Go for a walk and notice a detail that stands out. Question how it relates to your question.

o Journal about the question and what took place. As you repeat this exercise, you'll eventually discern the difference between a made-up and informative response.

Aligning with Flow through Creative Expression

Frequency: once a week and ongoing as wanted

Objective: to initiate flow and engage the unconscious

What matters most in a creative practice is not the chosen medium as much as your approach and attitude. Because I am most familiar with writing, movement, and drawing, I will use these. Feel free to apply the following approach to another medium.

o Gather paper, pens, music, or other materials you need and turn off your phone to prepare your space to be free of distractions.

o Devote a minimum of thirty minutes. Consider setting a timer.

o Sit quietly for five minutes. Empty your mind of thoughts and expectation. If any show up, let them float past without engaging with them. Follow how your breath causes your chest and belly to expand and contract.

o Writing: Write down the first word or phrase that arises and let it lead to consequent phrases and sentences. Welcome a stream of thoughts and feelings to spill onto the page. They need not make sense or be a consistent narrative. Consider associative meaning, sound, voice, and point of view. Write at a comfortable pace without stopping. Keep going as if the verbal stream is as natural as breath.

o Movement: Notice whatever small motion is already taking place in your body and amplify those movements. Stay in place or take up more space into the room. Engage the obvious parts of yourself like arms, legs, and torso, but remember also to engage fingers, toes, and belly. Let your body go and take the lead while you remain a neutral witness. Let your body take you into familiar and unfamiliar movements.

o Drawing: As soon as your pen (pencil, brush, etc.) contacts the paper, let it move across the space without concern for where it goes. Be guided by both the feeling of your hand, arm, and torso as well as the images appearing on the paper. Imagine the images appearing out from fog, though sometimes only the mist of fog appears.

o Notice what you notice. Watch for hesitations and exuberance, what's in the forefront of your awareness and the sidelines, the familiar and the unfamiliar, your criticisms and encouragements. Welcome play, improvisation, investigation, tangents, experimentation, order, and disorder. Censor none of it. Welcome what wants to show up. Get out of your way. Quiet the ego and critic. Continue until your time is up.

o Notice the difference in how you feel from before you began.

o Avoid judging or returning to the work to improve upon what you've created. Reflect upon your creation as genuine depiction of the moment. Return to it a day or a week later to see what reveals itself once you've established some distance.

Establishing a We

Frequency: once or as wanted

Objective: to shift out of a self-centered perspective into a collective perspective

Requirement: two people

This practice is likely to feel awkward given its unfamiliar perceiving process and shift in point of view. Grant yourself great leeway. Let go of the need to be correct or accurate.

o Sit across from your partner in a comfortable position.

o Briefly meditate for five minutes or so. Use whatever meditative practice you know, which may be as simple as focusing on the breath as described above. The idea here is to align with presence and not engage distracting thoughts.

o Set up a timer for ten minutes. One of you agrees to go first.

o One person speaks aloud what is being noticed using We as the pronoun. For example, "<u>We</u> see the clock on the wall." Or "We feel tired." Consider sensations, feelings, and thoughts that may originate in yourself or your partner. Consider what you perceive in the room. It's okay if what you say is being perceived is approximate or inaccurate.

o The other person listens as a witness.

o The speaker notices any difficulty and hesitancy in using We.

o Switch roles.

o Share about your experience and discuss.

o Option: Once familiar with this exercise, expand the We to include others—family, friends, and strangers—who are not present in the room.

Connecting with the Cosmos

Frequency: once or as wanted

Objective: to experience our planetary connected self

Our immediate surroundings provide ample stimuli to keep us occupied without ever having to look up or out. Extending the boundaries of our skin to sense the larger body opens us to a relationship and communication with nature and reinforces a sense of belonging. This exercise relies on imagination, but be open to receiving sensory impressions as well.

o At night, go someplace where stars are visible.

o Ground with the earth. Sit or stand. Feel gravity holding you in place. Feel your feet or any other part of you touching the skin of earth. Look at the shapes of whatever is nearby. Inhale what there is to smell. Listen to sounds around you.

o Close your eyes. Witness your senses shifting from outer to inner awareness. Welcome the inner quiet or noise and whatever else shows up on the screen of your attention.

o Imagine a stranger is doing this same activity from another location on Earth. That person sees you doing this practice. Imagine what they are perceiving and thinking about you.

o Send them a message in a whisper.

o Open your eyes and look up at the sky, clouds, and stars. Notice how far you can see.

o Imagine that the cosmos also sees and feels you. What does a star make of you? What is a forest whispering to you? What is the ocean saying? What nudge comes from wind or soil?

Notes

I. THE ROOTS OF BELIEFS

1. Blake, *Marriage of Heaven and Hell*, 36.
2. Campbell, *Reflections on the Art of Living*, 39.
3. Lewis, "It's Like This," 192.
4. Rees, "The Bereaved and Their Hallucinations."
5. Hanna, "What Is Somatics?" 341.
6. Solnit, "Acts of Hope."
7. United Nations Development Programme, "Global Multidimensional Index Report 2018."

2. AN INTEGRATION OF ENERGY HEALING

1. Kafatos, et al., "Biofield Science: Current Physics Perspectives."
2. Oschman, *Energy Medicine*, 8.
3. Dale, *The Subtle Body*, 166.
4. Merleau-Ponty, *The Primacy of Perception*, 162.
5. Cohen, *Sensing, Feeling and Action*, 5.
6. Tabatabaee, et al., "Effect of Therapeutic Touch," 142–47.
7. Duke Health, "What Is Integrative Medicine?"
8. Hellmann, "U.S. Health Care Ranked Worst."
9. Stephano, "Top 10 Medical Tourism Destinations."
10. Oschman, "What Is Healing," 179.
11. Gerber, *Vibrational Medicine*, 241.

12. Schwartz and Simon, *The Energy Healing Experiments,* 231.

13. Gustafson, "Barbara Dossey," 72–77.

14. Frankl, *Man's Search for Meaning,* 88.

15. Eisenstein, *Sacred Economics,* 6.

3. THE INTELLIGENCE OF INTUITIVE AND SOMATIC AWARENESS

1. World Health Organization, "Violence against Women."

2. Goldberg, "Why Women Are Poor at Science."

3. Gilligan, *In a Different Voice.*

4. American Psychological Association, "Individuals With Intersex Conditions."

5. From a review from *The British Critic* (April 1818).

6. "The 2019 VIDA Count."

7. Stewart, "Women Are Running for Office in Record Numbers."

8. Anderson and Adams, *Scaling Leadership,* 43–45.

9. The World Bank, "Missed Opportunities."

10. Women's World Banking, "The Impact of Microfinance on Women."

11. Martin, "We Are Becoming the Future," 198.

12. Born, *The Born Einstein Letters,* 89.

13. Salk, *Anatomy of Reality,* 79–80.

14. Roth, *Maps to Ecstasy,* 98.

15. Rehfeld et al., "Dance Training Is Superior."

16. Albani et al., "Feasibility of Home Exercises," 233–39.

17. Graham, *Blood Memory,* 139.

18. Barrett, *Secrets of Your Cells,* 58.

19. Karagulla and Kunz, *The Chakras and the Human Energy Field,* 28.

20. Dale, 236.

21. Popp, "Cancer Growth and Its Inhibition," 53–60.

22. Benor, "Distant Healing," 249.

23. Dossey, *One Mind,* xxv–xxvi.

24. Brennan, *Hands of Light,* 64.

4. THE ECOLOGY OF THE SELF

1. Hillman, *The Thought of the Heart and the Soul of the World,* 45.

2. Wolcott, "Love After Love," 328.

3. Cigna, "2018 Cigna U.S. Loneliness Index."

4. Kennedy, "Children Spend Half the Time Playing Outside."

5. Pearl, "Climate Despair Is Making People Give Up on Life."

6. Anxiety and Depression Association of America, "Facts and Statistics."

7. Whitman. "Song of Myself," 28.

8. Gaines, "Collision, Consciousness, and Community," 60.

9. Fox, "The Practice of Huayan Buddhism," 265.

10. Childre, et al., *Heart Intelligence*, 201.

11. Hainsworth, "The Effect of Geophysical Phenomena on Human Health."

12. Mitsutake, "Does Shumann Resonance Affect Our Blood Pressure?"

13. Williams, "Terry Tempest Williams: Erosion."

14. Moore, "Suzanne Simard Changed How the World Sees Trees."

15. Roszak, *The Voice of the Earth*, 14.

16. Estés, *Women Who Run with the Wolves*, 210.

17. Wohlleben, *The Hidden Life of Trees*, viii.

18. Haviland, "Guugu Yimithirr Cardinal Directions," 25–47.

19. Witkin and Goodenough, *Cognitive Styles, Essence, and Origins*.

20. James, *The Varieties of Religious Experience*, 308.

5. THE EMBODIMENT OF EXPANDED PERCEPTIONS

1. Morrison, "No Place for Self-Pity, No Room for Fear."

2. Zaltman, *How Customers Think*.

3. Lispector, *Aqua Viva*, 17.

4. Fraleigh, *Dancing Identity*, 56–57.

5. Park, et al., "The Physiological Effects of Shinrin-Yoku," 18–26.

6. Childre, et al., *The HeartMath Solution*, 14.

7. Hannaford, *Playing in the Unified Field*, 56–57.

8. Gladwell, *The Tipping Point*.

9. Rensselaer Polytechnic Institute, "Minority Rules."

10. McCraty, et al., "The Global Coherence Initiative," 64–77.

11. Bourgeault, *Eye of the Heart*, 24.

12. Sagan, *Cosmos*, 244.

13. Wilber, *Integral Meditation*, 14–15.

6. A WAY FORWARD

1. Dispenza, *Breaking the Habit of Being Yourself,* 53.

2. Thomas and Kim, "Lost Touch? Implications of Physical Touch for Physical Health."

Bibliography

American Psychological Association, "Individuals with Intersex Conditions." American Psychological Association (website). Accessed January 4, 2020.

Anderson, Robert J. and William A. Adams. *Scaling Leadership: Building Organization Capability and Capacity to Create Outcomes that Matter Most.* Hoboken, N.J.: John Wiley & Sons, Inc., 2019.

Anxiety and Depression Association of America. "Facts and Statistics." Anxiety and Depression Association of America (website). Accessed January 21, 2019.

Barrett, Sondra. *Secrets of Your Cells: Discovering Your Body's Inner Intelligence.* Boulder, Colo.: Sounds True, 2013.

Benor, Daniel J. "Distant Healing." *Subtle Energies & Energy Medicine* 11, no. 3 (April 20, 2013). Accessed February 1, 2019.

Blake, William. *Marriage of Heaven and Hell.* New York: Dover Publications, 1994.

Born, Max. *The Born Einstein Letters.* New York: Macmillan Press, 1971.

Bourgeault, Cynthia. *Eye of the Heart: A Spiritual Journey into the Imaginal Realm.* Boston: Shambhala, 2020.

Brennan, Barbara. *Hands of Light: A Guide to Healing through the Human Energy Field.* New York: Bantam Books, 1988.

Campbell, Joseph. *Reflections on the Art of Living.* New York: HarperPerennial, 1995.

Childre, Doc, Howard Martin, Deborah Rozman, and Rollin McCraty. *Heart Intelligence: Connecting with the Intuitive Guidance of the Heart.* Cardiff by the Sea, Calif.: Waterfront Digital Press, 2017.

Childre, Doc, Howard Martin, and Donna Beech. *The HeartMath Solution: The Institute of HeartMath's Revolutionary Program for Engaging the Power of the Heart's Intelligence*. New York: Harper One, 2000.

Cigna. "2018 Cigna U.S. Loneliness Index: Survey of 2000 Americans Examining Behaviors Driving Loneliness in the United States." Cigna (website). Accessed December 14, 2019.

Cohen, Bonnie Bainbridge. *Sensing, Feeling, and Action: The Experiential Anatomy of Body-Mind Centering*. Berkley, Calif.: North Atlantic Books, 1993.

Dale, Cyndi. *The Subtle Body: An Encyclopedia of Your Energetic Anatomy*. Boulder, Colo.: Sounds True, 2009.

Dispenza, Joe. *Breaking the Habit of Being Yourself: How to Lose Your Mind and Create a New One*. Carlsbad, Calif.: Hay House, 2012.

Dossey, Larry, M.D. *One Mind: How Our Individual Mind Is Part of a Greater Consciousness and Why It Matters*. Carlsbad, Calif.: Hay House, 2013.

Duke Health. "What Is Integrative Medicine?" Duke Health (website). Accessed January 26, 2020.

Eisenstein, Charles. *Sacred Economics: Money, Gift, and Society in the Age of Transition*. Berkley, Calif.: North Atlantic Books, 2011.

Estés, Clarissa Pinkola. *Women Who Run with the Wolves: Myths and Stories of the Wild Woman Archetype*. New York: Ballantine Books, 2003.

Albani, Giovanni, Giuseppe Veneziano, Clara Lunardon, Calogero Vinci, Alessandra Daniele, Federico Cossa, and Alessandro Mauro. "Feasibility of Home Exercises to Enhance the Benefits of Tango Dancing in People with Parkinson's Disease." *Complementary Therapies in Medicine* 42 (February 2019): 233–39.

Fox, Alan. "The Practice of Huayan Buddhism." *Semantic Scholar* (2015): 265. Accessed January 5, 2020.

Fraleigh, Sondra Horton. *Dancing Identity: Metaphysics in Motion*. Pittsburgh, Pa.: University of Pittsburgh Press, 2004.

Frankl, Victor. *Man's Search for Meaning*. New York: Pocket Books, 2006.

Gaines, Andrew. "Collision, Consciousness, and Community." *Contact Quarterly*. Summer/Fall, 1995.

Gerber, Richard. *Vibrational Medicine: The #1 Handbook of Subtle-Energy Therapies*. Rochester, Vt.: Bear & Company, 2001.

Gilligan, Carol. *In a Different Voice: Psychological Theory and Women's Development*. Cambridge, Mass.: Harvard University Press, 2016.

Gladwell, Malcolm. *The Tipping Point: How Little Things Can Make a Big Difference.* New York: Back Bay Books, 2002.

Goldberg, Suzanne. "Why Women Are Poor at Science, by Harvard President." *The Guardian.* January 18, 2005. Accessed January 27, 2020.

Graham, Martha. *Blood Memory.* New York: Doubleday, 1991.

Gustafson, Craig. "Barbara Dossey, Ph.D., RN: Developing a Healing Approach in Nursing." *Integrative Medicine* 14, no. 5 (October 2015): 72–77. Accessed June 12, 2020.

Hainsworth, L. B. "The Effect of Geophysical Phenomena on Human Health." *Speculations in Science and Technology* 6, no. 5 (1983): 439–44. Accessed October 3, 2020.

Hanna, Thomas. "What Is Somatics?" In *Bone, Breath & Gesture: Practices of Embodiment,* edited by Don Hanlon Johnson. Berkeley, Calif.: North Atlantic Books, 1995.

Hannaford, Carla. *Playing in the Unified Field: Raising and Becoming Conscious, Creative Human Beings.* Salt Lake City: Great River Books, 2010.

Haviland, John B. "Guugu Yimithirr Cardinal Directions" *Ethos* 26, no. 1 (March 1998): 25–47.

Hellmann, Melissa. "U.S. Health Care Ranked Worst in the Developed World," *Time.* June 17, 2014. Accessed January 25, 2019.

Hillman, James. *The Thought of the Heart and the Soul of the World.* Dallas: Spring Publishing, 1981.

James, William. *The Varieties of Religious Experience.* Cambridge, Mass.: Harvard University Press, 1985.

Kafatos, Menas C., Gaétan Chevalier, Ph.D., Deepak Chopra, M.D., John Hubacher, M.D., Subhash Kak, Ph.D., Neil D. Theise, M.D. "Biofield Science: Current Physics Perspectives." *Global Advances in Health and Medicine* 1, suppl. (October 30, 2018): 25–34. Accessed September 5, 2020.

Karagulla, Shafica and Dora Van Gelder Kunz. *The Chakras and the Human Energy Field.* Wheaton, Ill.: Quest Books, 1989.

Kennedy, Rebecca. "Children Spend Half the Time Playing Outside in Comparison to Their Parents." Child in the City (website). January 15, 2018. Accessed December 14, 2019.

Kübler-Ross, Elizabeth. *On Death and Dying.* New York: Scribner, 1993.

Lewis, Wendy. "It's Like This." In *What Book!? Buddha Poems from Beat to Hiphop,* edited by Gary Gach. Berkeley, Calif.: Parallax Press, 1998.

Lispector, Clarice. *Aqua Viva.* New York: New Directions, 2012.

Martin, Stephan. "We Are Becoming the Future: An Interview with Barbara Max Hubbard." In *Cosmic Conversations: Dialogues on the Nature of the Universe and the Search for Reality,* 189–204. New York: Red Wheel Weiser, 2009.

McCraty, Rollin, Annette Deyhle, Ph.D., and Doc Childre. "The Global Coherence Initiative: Creating a Coherent Planetary Standing Wave." *Global Advanced Health Medicine* 1, no. 1 (March 1, 2012): 64–77.

Merleau-Ponty, Maurice. *The Primacy of Perception: And Other Essays on Phenomenological Psychology, the Philosophy of Art, History, and Politics.* Evanston, Ill.: Northwestern University Press, 1964.

Mindell, Arnold. *Working on Yourself Alone: Inner Dreambody Work.* Portland, Ore.: Lao Tse Press, 1991.

Mitsutake, G., K. Otsuka, M. Hayakawa, M. Sekiguchi, G. Cornélissen, F. Halberg. "Does Schumann Resonance Affect Our Blood Pressure?" *Biomedicine and Pharmacotherapy* 59, Suppl. 1 (October 2005): S10–S14.

Moore, Robert. "Suzanne Simard Changed How the World Sees Trees." *New York Magazine,* May 6, 2021. Accessed September 12, 2021.

Morrison Toni. "No Place for Self-Pity, No Room for Fear." *The Nation,* April 6, 2015.

Oschman, James L. *Energy Medicine: The Scientific Basis.* Dover, N.H.: Elsevier, 2016.

Oschman. "What is healing energy? Part 3: silent pulses," *Journal of Bodywork and Movement Therapies* 13, no. 3 (1997).

Pallant, Cheryl. *Contact Improvisation: An Introduction to a Vitalizing Dance Form.* Jefferson, N.C.: McFarland and Company, 2006.

Park, Bum Jin, Yuko Tsunetsugu, Tamami Kasetani, Takahide Kagawa, and Yoshifumi Miyazaki. "The Physiological Effects of Shinrin-Yoku (Taking in the Forest Atmosphere or Forest Bathing): Evidence from Field Experiments in 24 Forests across Japan." *Environmental Health and Preventive Medicine* 15 (May 5, 2009): 18–26.

Pearl, Mike. "Climate Despair Is Making People Give Up on Life" *Vice.* July 11, 2019.

Popp, Fritz-Albert. "Cancer Growth and Its Inhibition in Terms of Coherence." *Electromagnetic Biology and Medicine* 28, no. 1 (July 7, 2009).

Rees, W. D. "The Bereaved and Their Hallucinations." In *Bereavement: Its Psychosocial Aspects,* edited by Bernard Schoenberg, Austin H. Kutscher, and Arthur C. Carr. New York: Columbia University Press, 1975.

Rehfeld, Kathrin, Angie Lüders, Anita Hökelmann, Volkmar Lessmann, Joern Kaufmann, Tanja Brigadski, Patrick Müller, and Notger G. Müller. "Dance Training Is Superior to Repetitive Physical Exercise in Inducing Brain Plasticity in the Elderly." *PLOS One* 13, no. 7 (July 11, 2018). Accessed March 5, 2020.

Rensselaer Polytechnic Institute. "Minority Rules: Scientists Discover Tipping Point for the Spread of Ideas." Phys.org (website) (July 25, 2011). Accessed June 21, 2020.

Roszak, Theodore. *The Voice of the Earth: An Exploration of Ecopsychology.* New York: Red Wheel/Weiser, 2001.

Roth, Gabrielle. *Maps to Ecstasy: The Healing Power of Movement.* Novato, Calif.: New World Library, 1998.

Sagan, Carl. *Cosmos.* Ballantine, N.Y.: Ballantine Books, 2013.

Salk, Jonas. *Anatomy of Reality: Merging of Intuition and Reason.* New York: Columbia University Press, 1983.

Schwartz, Gary and William L. Simon. *The Energy Healing Experiments: Science Reveals Our Natural Power to Heal.* New York: Atria Books, 2007.

Sewall, Laura. "On Beauty and the Brain." In *Ecopsychology: Science, Totems, and the Technological Species,* edited by Peter H. Kahn Jr. and Patricia H. Hasbach. Cambridge, Mass.: MIT Press, 2012.

Solnit, Rebecca. "Acts of Hope," *Orion.* Accessed December 2, 2021.

Stephano, Renée-Marie. "Top 10 Medical Tourism Destinations in the World" *Medical Tourism Magazine.* Accessed January 29, 2019.

Stewart, Emily. "Women Are Running for Office in Record Numbers. In Corporate America, They're Losing Ground." Vox (website). June 8, 2018.

Tabatabaee, Amir, Mansoureh Zagheri Tafreshi, Maryam Rassouli, Seyed Amir Aledavood, Hamid AlaviMajd, and Seyed Kazem Farahmand. "Effect of Therapeutic Touch in Patients with Cancer: a Literature Review." *Medical Archives* 70, no. 2 (April 2016): 142–47. Accessed July 14, 2019.

Thomas, Patricia A. and Seoyoun Kim. "Lost Touch? Implications of Physical Touch for Physical Health." *The Journals of Gerontology, Series B* 76, no. 3 (March 2021): e111–e115. Accessed September 21, 2020.

"The 2019 Vida Count." VIDA: Women in the Arts (website). Accessed January 10, 2023.

United Nations Development Programme. "Global Multidimensional Index Report 2018." UNDP Human Development Reports (website). Accessed January 24, 2020.

Women's World Banking. "The Impact of Microfinance on Women and Economic Development: A Client Study." Women's World Banking (website) (October 7, 2010). Accessed July 13, 2019.

The World Bank. "Missed Opportunities: The High Cost of Not Educating Girls." The World Bank (website) (July 11, 2018). Accessed July 19, 2019.

World Health Organization. "Violence against Women." World Health Organization (website) (November 29, 2017). Accessed May 30, 2019.

Wilber, Ken. *Integral Meditation: Mindfulness as a Path to Grow Up, Wake Up, and Show Up in Your Life.* Boulder, Colo.: Shambhala, 2016.

Whitman, Walt. "Song of Myself" in *Leaves of Grass.* New York: Penguin Books, 2005.

Williams, Terry Tempest. "Terry Tempest Williams: Erosion." Bioneers.org (website) (2019). Accessed January 25, 2020.

Witkin, Herman and Donald R. Goodenough. *Cognitive Styles, Essence, and Origins: Field Dependence and Field Independence.* Madison, Conn.: International Universities Press Inc., 1981.

Wohlleben, Peter. *The Hidden Life of Trees: What They Feel, How They Communicate—Discoveries from a Secret World.* Vancouver, B.C.: Greystone Books, 2016.

Wolcott, Derek. "Love After Love" in *Collected Poems: 1948–1984.* New York: Farrar, Straus, and Giroux, 1987.

Zaltman, Gerald. *How Customers Think: Essential Insights into the Mind of the Market.* Boston: Harvard Business School Press, 2003.

Index